10-20-21

I
WANT
TO
BELIEVE

FINDING YOUR WAY IN AN AGE OF MANY FAITHS

MEL LAWRENZ

Regal

From Gospel Light
Ventura, California, U.S.A.

Published by Regal
From Gospel Light
Ventura, California, U.S.A.
www.regalbooks.com
Printed in the U.S.A.

Library of Congress Cataloging-in-Publication Data
Lawrenz, Mel.
  I want to believe : finding your way in an age of many faiths / Mel Lawrenz.
     p. cm.
  ISBN 978-0-8307-4452-7 (hard cover)
  1. Apologetics. 2. Belief and doubt. 3. Christianity and other religions. I. Title.
  BT1103.L39 2007
  239—dc22
                                                                    2007011629

1 2 3 4 5 6 7 8 9 10 / 10 09 08 07

Rights for publishing this book outside the U.S.A. or in non-English languages are administered by Gospel Light Worldwide, an international not-for-profit ministry. For additional information, please visit www.glww.org, email info@glww.org, or write to Gospel Light Worldwide, 1957 Eastman Avenue, Ventura, CA 93003, U.S.A.

Contents

I Want to Believe, and I'm Not Ashamed of It

My daughter's voice on the phone was clipped and urgent. "Dad, I need you to come outside right *now*!"

"Eva? Where *are* you?"

"In the driveway. Please come outside right *now*!"

Her voice was on the edge of teenage emergency frequency, so I slammed the phone down and ran outside to see her standing next to her '95 Honda Civic hatchback, a look of panic on her face. Then I saw why. Smoke was billowing out of the front and side edges of the car's engine compartment.

"What happened?" I snapped, as I popped the hood and, standing back, flipped it open. Now the smoke rose out of the engine compartment like a column, and I was sure that from a block or two away it must have had a mushroom shape to it.

"Well, it started to act and smell funny as I was driving home."

"What about the gauges inside?"

"Yeah, they were pretty high."

By now the stench of burnt rubber had stung my nostrils, and I was already calculating in my head the cost of a new engine.

"Well, Eva, how far back did the car start to 'act funny'?"

"Oh, I'd say, up on Capitol Drive."

Now I knew that Capitol Drive was a good three miles from where the barbecued car now sat in our driveway.

"Well, what did it sound like? Did you get any clue that something was terribly wrong? Did the car sound funny?"

"Yes, it did."

"Well, *what* did it sound like?"

She thought for a moment, not like an auto mechanic, but like a poet (which she is) looking for just the right expression.

"Like a thousand metal butterflies all flying at once."

I was speechless—it was a perfect expression. I could just imagine it. How would you describe a cacophony of ticking and clacking coming from an engine compartment? But my admiration for the metaphor quickly dissipated.

"A thousand metal butterflies? Well, Eva, what is the threshold where you would have pulled off the road? Ten thousand metal butterflies? A hundred thousand metal butterflies?" I wanted her to hear the intense irritation in my voice, but I also really wanted to know. Would the engine have to blow up, sending the hood flying in the air, for her to pull over and realize there was a genuine auto emergency in the works?

She smiled in that way that teenage girls soften the hearts of their fathers—though I tried to maintain as firm a heart as possible before launching into my lecture on how not to fry your car, and kicking myself for not giving the lecture a long time ago.

Now here is what I learned: My dear teenage daughter, who had never had anything go wrong with a car before and did not know the special emergency nature of an overheated engine, knew that something was wrong. The sound of "a thousand metal butterflies all flying at once" told her that. But she didn't know the *meaning* of the sound. And she didn't know the clicking, chattering, clapping sound coming from the engine was a sign that destruction was at hand.

Most people I talk to know that there is something wrong in life. Headlines about wars and famines and muggings spell that out. On a personal level, some people know there is something wrong in their lives, because they've been to the funeral home or their doctor has sent them to a specialist or they signed the final divorce papers. And people who haven't been to any of these places are at least hearing something strange and disturbing in the air—something like a thousand metal butterflies—but they don't know what is making the noise and they don't know *what it means*.

That is one reason why we keep looking for God. And it is one reason why we want to believe. I know it's one of the main reasons I want to believe.

Of all the things that drive us, the strongest is the drive to believe. We might think that hunger is our strongest impulse . . . or sex, or greed or war. And it certainly is true that an empty stomach or a member of the opposite sex or a gambling table or a nice case of bloodlust can easily become the obsession *du jour*. But there is something deep inside us that keeps churning and seeking and reaching and probing and crying out. Oftentimes it is the disturbing sense that something is terribly wrong, because from some hidden place (stuck in your head, twisting your stomach, shaking your soul) comes the sound of a thousand metal butterflies. Sometimes it feels like an emptiness, sometimes like an ache.

That's the drive to believe. How else can we explain the surging interest of so many people today to find spiritual answers and spiritual anchoring when everything else in the world seems so uncertain?

Sometimes it's the funeral that prompts us to want to believe. What happens when we cross that line? Will I ever see my loved ones again? Am I supposed to be doing something now that will make a difference then?

Sometimes it's the desire to be forgiven that drives us toward God. What do we do with a load of guilt that feels like a tumor lodged beneath our rib cage? Is there a God who can silence the screaming of accusers? And is God willing to? Will I ever see justice—real justice—when everything is sorted out?

We are born believers. It's just simply how we're made. That's why full-grown adults need to look at small children in order to learn what real faith looks like. It's why Jesus said that the central qualifier for someone who wants to live under the protection and provision of the kingdom of God is that he or she have "faith like a child" (see Matt. 18:3-4; Mark 10:15; Luke 18:17).

Children know things that we adults talk ourselves out of. They know they have to believe in a parent, in the certainty of blankets, in teachers who can be trusted to tell the truth—not just because it's convenient, but because it's the only thing that makes sense. Children believe in God even without formal instruction, and they assume there is a moral fabric to the universe. "That's not fair!" can mean "Bobby stole my toy," but it also is an affirmation of faith: "There is moral structure in the universe!" There is a reason why a child asks where his or her cat or dog is when it dies.

This is why the human race has never been able to talk itself out of believing in God—as hard as it has tried. It just doesn't make sense not to believe in God. Usually, when a person does succeed in suppressing that deepest drive or in putting blinders on so as not to see this reality brighter than the sun straight above, it is usually achieved by latching onto some kind of God substitute. If we don't believe there is a God over heaven and Earth, we'll make someone or something in our lives the next-best kind of god. And we'll probably continue to keep on looking for the Real Thing anyway.

When I turned 27, I was ready for a booster shot of faith. It was a strange set of circumstances and quite unexpected. On my twenty-seventh birthday, I realized that I had reached an age that my father never had. He died of sudden pneumonia that overwhelmed him as he sat in an easy chair at home. He had been around the sun 26 times, but just didn't get around one more time. Had just started adult life, really.

As I approached my twenty-seventh birthday, I had this strange feeling that I was about to cross a definitive line—like when an explorer marks the place that is the farthest reach of the previous explorer and then takes one more step into new territory—off the map, over the edge and no turning back. There was nothing at all pleasant about this sensation: It was frightening and lonely and I was embarrassed by it, so I hardly told anybody.

To be more exact, I felt like I was living on borrowed time, like I had gone farther in life than I should have. A 20-something man shouldn't be older than his own father. I shouldn't reach an age when I'd think of my own father as a kid. I derived no view of a heavenly Father through him.

I was too young, and he was too possessed by alcohol and hedonism anyway.

When my wife and I had children, I was already fearing for them. What if I left them when they were two or four years old, which was how old my sister and I were when our father died? What could I do to stop pneumonia or cancer or a plane crash? What commitments can I make? Is there anything much in life I have control over? Is there any guarantee that I can impart to them a sense of purpose and connection with their heavenly Father so that the part of their soul that I could never reach as a parent would be filled with the love of God?

I came to believe that this sense of mortality—which is still vivid to me now with another 25 years having passed and my kids in college—is a good thing. Why should we not feel mortal? We *are*. This is not morbid—it's just real.

It drove me to want to believe. And that's a very good thing. When we believe—really believe by seeking, probing, reading, studying, discovering, consulting, reflecting, studying some more, adjusting, discarding, testing, building, inventing, then rejecting invention—when we believe like that, it feels okay to be off into an undiscovered country. Way off the map. This must be what drives explorers. They must fear the deep blue and the undiscovered tribe in the next valley and the first space walk, but they are carried along by something they believe in.

We are driven to believe for all kinds of reasons, not least of which is the unavoidable reality of God. When you're standing in the jungle and hear a great roar, you can't help but stare and squint to find the big cat—for a moment anyway. And then you don't stand around and debate whether you believe in the existence of tigers because in a book somewhere you read about the prominent use of tigers in mythologies. You hear the roar, and then you *do something* about it. Whenever we confront a reality so much bigger, so much more powerful than ourselves, we naturally wonder how the realization of this presence should affect our actions. Reaction seems a necessity. Is there a tiger there in the jungle? Better run. Is there a God somewhere in the world? Better bow.

Another major reason we want to believe is because God made us that way—as a life necessity. The sensation of hunger prompts us to seek food, so we stoke the furnace of the body with fuel that it needs to survive and thrive. At a much higher level, our drive to believe keeps us looking for God. Saint Augustine, who sixteen centuries ago wrote the most famous spiritual autobiography of all time, opened *The Confessions* with the following proposition (actually, a heartfelt prayer offered to God): "Everlasting God, in whom we live and move and have our being: You have made us for Yourself, and our hearts are restless until they find their rest in You." Untold millions of people have found that single sentence to ring as true for them as anything else in life. For some people, that restlessness is the pain of loneliness or shame or waywardness. For others the restlessness is an ache deep inside—a feeling and a thought that there must be something more, a higher purpose, a higher Person. Restlessness is not a bad thing, if it propels us toward something that keeps us alive and causes us to flourish.

We also have a drive to believe because we are always looking for a structure of meaning and morality for life. We want something solid beneath our feet—some kind of foundation of truth on which we can base real convictions.

And then we want to have definition to our convictions, and connections between the pieces—like a house we can live in, with walls and rooms and a roof over our heads to protect us from the elements. Opinion forming is like taking a stroll on a path. Faith building is like building a home you can live in.

We are intellectually driven not just to believe one or two things but many convictions and sub-convictions that may start out as rubbery opinion but become firm belief—"doctrine" in the best sense of the word. None of us want anyone to ever say of us, "Older, but no wiser." Wise people believe. They know that belief is the wellspring of wisdom. Their wisdom is their security—not an arrogant sense of possessing God, but of being possessed by God. Not bigotry, but belonging. The one certain path to living the life of the fool is to work as hard as we can to suppress the drive to believe.

There is a story in chapter 9 of the Gospel of Mark in which a desperate man came to Jesus (see also Matt.17:14-18; Luke 9:38-43). The man's son was subject to horrible convulsions. He'd turn mute, fall to the ground and lapse into unconsciousness. His body was bruised and scarred. This had been going on for years, and his father felt helpless and hopeless. He had passing thoughts that maybe his son would be better off dead than living under this domination. And so when the father heard rumors about a man capable of performing miracles, he thought, *Why not? What have I got to lose?* He brought his son to Jesus.

"What's wrong with your son?"

"He convulses. He's thrown to the ground. He's fallen into fires and into water."

"How long?"

"A long time—since childhood. I brought him to Your disciples, but they couldn't do anything. If You can do anything, take pity on us and help us."

And Jesus had one question: "*If? . . . If I can? . . . Everything is possible for anyone who believes*" (see v. 23).

Now, just pause there. If you were the man, what would be the very next thing out of your mouth? A miracle worker has engaged you in conversation. He's sized up your dilemma. He's said that anything can happen. That there is no reason to give up hope. That there is a stronger power.

Wouldn't you be tempted just to play up to the miracle worker? To say whatever it was you thought he wanted you to say? Just get him to wave the wand or whatever he does and see what happens?

But this father looked at Jesus and with unvarnished honesty said, "*I do believe; help me overcome my unbelief!*" (v. 24, emphasis added). I find that statement stunning. What was that man saying?

When a person can look to God and say, "I do believe; help me with my unbelief," he or she has actually said, "With as much as I know and as much as I have experienced and as much evidence as I have, I know that God is real, and He is good, and He is powerful, and He is here. I believe God knows; I believe God acts. But . . . there is so much I think I should believe that is beyond my reach and beyond my trust. My faith gets me just so far. I'm afraid if I go too far out on a limb, it will just break off. I fear that my desire to believe some things that would be wonderful are just wishful thinking on my part. And I don't want to look like a fool. I don't want to be taken in. If I believe in and worship God, I want to know this God is real. So God, in all honesty, this is me:

I do believe, and I think there is more I should believe but I have not been able to believe. Help me. I want to believe."

I used to think that God is only pleased when we say to Him, "I do believe." But having lived a little longer and having watched many more people running and stumbling and thrashing their way through life, and having read the Bible with a somewhat more careful eye, I think God is pleased when someone says, "I want to believe." Sometimes that's the best we can come up with. This isn't a paltry offering. Wanting to believe is much more than stumbling aimlessly. It is a steady walk down a path that you may be able to see only to the next turn, but when you can glimpse a proper horizon, a God-ward horizon, you know you're headed in the right direction. Each step becomes more certain because you can see where you're going. Your beliefs ring true, and they start to form a harmony.

Wanting to believe is what gets us to believing, and believing well.

And there is really only one explanation for where the *want* comes from. It's got to be a divine allure, an inherent attractiveness in God. Because of the way things usually go in life, there are all kinds of reasons why my next *want* would be for something merely physical, something I can stick a fork into or something that will make my body tingle. And there are lots of "want suppressors," disappointments that should make all of us cynical and cold. But unless we've chosen total hedonism or complete skepticism, we still want to believe. This is a gift. Most people seem to know that religious and sectarian wars shouldn't give God a bad name. They shouldn't be a reason to give up on believing. God is not to blame for the bad behavior of the human race.

There are few words in the Bible that hit me more strongly than "grace." The root meaning of "grace" is "attractiveness" or "beauty" (so we say a certain woman possesses a lot of grace or a young dancer is graceful in her movements). But a higher meaning of "grace" is "generosity." To talk about the grace of God is to speak of His "givingness" (if that were a word). God creates and loves and forgives and protects and leads because He gives. And then He gives again. And it doesn't stop. God guides and feeds and teaches and corrects and delivers us from evil. The only limit to God's givingness is our limitation in accepting it. Now this kind of generosity is inherently attractive. Grace as attractiveness; grace as gift. No wonder we want to believe. And we want to believe even when life's disappointments and injuries make it hard to believe. It is a rough world. We know that; God knows that. But we are better off living in a suffering world and having faith in God than suffering alone. Does that mean believing is just wishful thinking on our part, solace sought in superstition? No, we believe because of the irrepressible allure of the divine, and because there are good rational reasons to believe. These reasons are central to our explorations in this book.

But where does this allure take us? Where does the drive carry us?

Here is where we need to be careful. Our deepest drive may, if misdirected and uninformed, take us almost anywhere. Several years ago a very popular TV drama was centered on the obsessive drive of an FBI agent who had to find the truth. But not the conventional kind of truths FBI agents typically root out, like "Who did the bank robbery, and where is he now?" This story's protagonist, Fox Mulder, was assigned to the "X-Files," cases that ranged outside the normal to the paranormal and even to the supernatural. Somebody had to check out rumors of evil spells, demonic manifestations, hauntings and aliens on the loose. In the story, stretched out over nine seasons, Mulder was driven by one deeply personal ambition: to find out what happened to his younger sister on the night she was snatched out of their house by what seemed to be alien abductors. The slogan of *The X-Files* was "The truth is out there."

On the wall of his office, above his desk, hung a poster with a picture of a flying saucer above some treetops, a classic amateur picture of a UFO, with these words in big block letters: I WANT TO BELIEVE.

Maybe you've only heard news reports or read sensationalist tabloids about people who believe in alien abductions. But I once worked with a guy who really believed in them. More than that, he actually claimed he had been abducted on numerous occasions. We worked together on the grounds crew at a golf course. He was the mower. He was the quiet guy riding the big hovering mower out to do the fine work on the greens. Hardly ever said a word. Did a meticulous job on the greens. Was quick as a wizard on the big tractor mower down the fairways. And then one day in an article in the local newspaper, I saw his whole story and his reports of his abductions. In the interview, he detailed what you see when you're taking a night's ride in an alien's saucer (and I think his wife was along for the rides, too). Well, I was just a high schooler working on the golf course for the summer, and this whole thing felt too creepy to me, so I never asked him about it. Besides, I also watched him cutting those fairways on that fast tractor with a hundred razor-sharp cutters that sent clippings flying high in the air every which way, and I was frequently nearby, bent over planting petunias or something. He was not a man I wanted to antagonize.

Getting back to Fox Mulder of *The X-Files*: He wanted to believe what other people find difficult because he knew there may be all kinds of things in life that are unbelievable just because they are so completely out of the ordinary. But who ever said that everything that is real is ordinary? Or that the main criteria for us believing anything is because it can be labeled "ordinary"?

In contrast to Mulder's search for truth, his female FBI partner always wore a reminder of Christian faith: a small gold cross always laying lightly on her neck—a shiny little thing in what was otherwise a pretty gray story. Is such a cross the most ordinary thing in the world? Or is believing in a crucified Jesus—not just believing that He was killed, but that His death is worth wearing around your neck—the most extraordinary choice any human being can make?

Be careful about believing. You may get carried away. Actually, the things that really are worth believing in will carry you away. Believing in God is not like a scientist trapping an animal in a cage to bring back to the laboratory for further study and tests. So if you ever take a class or read a book in which the teacher or author is putting the idea of God under a microscope like a bug, then you know that person can't possibly be looking at the real thing.

God carries us away. He bears us up when we are crippled. He holds us up when we are weary. He cradles us when we're an hour old and in the last hour of our lives. He transports us into a future that we cannot possibly know.

But should you believe that anymore than that you'll get picked up tonight by some aliens offering you a joyride for the evening? There is a difference.

I want to believe. I know I do. And I know it's not just because of wishful thinking. Believing is our deepest drive, and this desire does lead to truth as long as it doesn't get twisted along the way. I'll even admit that there was a part of me that wanted to believe that the man who mowed the golf course really did have friends in really high places and that one day we'd sit down and he'd give me the whole inside story, detail by detail. But it was a very small part of me that wanted to believe that—I knew I couldn't believe that, because I knew it was groundless.

The way we believe and what we believe may carry us into a place in life where God is the indisputable benevolent king or carry us into fantasy or even delusion.

True believers abound.

CHAPTER 2

Why God Wants Us to Believe

There was a time when I thought that the reason I should believe was just because it is the right and proper thing to do. A kind of religious good manners. What civilized people do. A socially acceptable way to live in my culture, because most people I knew believed in God. Most people don't really want to stand out from the crowd when it comes to religious belief. It's one thing to stand out because you have a penchant for wearing distinctive shoes or because you're not afraid to tell people about the oddball movies you really like. But it is far more serious to tell people what your real spiritual convictions are—especially if you have none.

So many people say they believe, but all it amounts to is that somewhere in their conscience there is a small voice that says, "Nice people believe in God. It is proper to believe in God."

There was a time when I believed in God largely for that reason. But I think I knew deep down that my faith was as flimsy as a house of cards. And now I look back and shudder to think what the Creator of the universe and Master of heaven and Earth must have thought about my mannerly deference to Him. Is this kind of "faith" a positive stepping stone to something higher and more real, or is it so pitiful and so disrespectful of God and the truth that it really counts for nothing at all?

Perhaps it doesn't matter to God whether we come to Him from the void of atheism or from the paper, glue and crayon house of polite spirituality. What matters is whether we come to Him or not. If we give credence to Jesus' story about the prodigal son who returns home to the father who is ready to forgive all the waste and profligate living, then we can believe that what really matters is that we come back home to God to live and flourish in His family—however we get there.

Why does God want us to believe? I find that it is far easier for me to understand faith if I think of it that way around, rather than asking, *Why should we believe?* If we put the question the second way, then we will come up with a dozen different reasons to believe in God that may be as airy and meaningless as the reason of social politeness. And the focus will be on us: why *we* should believe. It's hard to get a clear vision of God when we're focusing on ourselves. When we're looking for a reliable doctor to diagnose and treat us, the real thing we are looking for is a good doctor. The search is not about the search. If we let discussions about our spirituality never get beyond spirituality, we've missed the point: Our spiritual drive is trying to move us toward God. That's like reading a book about cuisine that talks about hunger but doesn't describe food. A good book about food makes you salivate—not for another book, but for some *food*.

So when we ask the question this way: *Why does* God *want us to believe?* we are letting the lion roar for Himself.

Why does God want us to believe? What follows is a summary of some of the main ideas we find spread across the Bible, in both the Old and New Testaments.

Reason #1

A Creator God who went through all the trouble to create the universe and each of us in it cares deeply about what He has created.

There are, of course, parents who bear children and then have no regard for them. But the way things ought to be, and most of the time are, is that parents go through this amazing experience of bringing a new human being into the world, and then they usually care a great deal about what happens next. They will spend an extraordinary amount of time feeding and cleaning the child, providing a safe home and a comfortable place to sleep through the night. They will take the child to a doctor when sick, to school when it is time to begin a life of education, and to dance classes and clarinet lessons and athletic matches. Parents will weep for their kids when they make horrible choices, and they will applaud every significant achievement. Good parents will know that they cannot make their kids' choices for them, and they must not try to live vicariously through them.

And so God loves what He has created. The analogy of parent and child cannot begin to measure up to the love that God has for His offspring. I'm not sure whether Jesus intended to put a scowl or a smile on the faces of His listeners when He said, "Which of you, if his son asks for bread, will give him a stone? Or if he asks for a fish, will give him a snake?" (Matt. 7:9-10). And then comes the arrow: "If you, then, though you are evil, know how to give good gifts to your children, how much more will your Father in heaven give good gifts to those who ask him!" (v. 11).

Now there are belief systems that include a generic Creator of the universe who lacks specific personal attributes like intentionality, intellect and love. God is viewed as an "it." Those who in all honesty only come so far as to admit to an "it" that put in motion the beginning of the universe with design (like Albert Einstein) are at least saying that all the evidence negates the feeble notion that the only thing that exists is matter. Believing that there must be a Creator of all things puts us in the position of wanting to know what can be known about this Creator. Believing makes us want to believe more and prompts us to truly search. And while the skeptic may say that this is the slippery slope down which multitudes of people have tumbled into deeper levels of self-delusion and (of course) the worst kind of psychological and sociological pathology, that still hasn't stopped most people in most parts of the world from wanting to know more about creation and Creator. (Unless you believe only in nature and not in any God who created nature, like the former premier of the U.S.S.R. Mikhail Gorbachev, who said, "I believe in the cosmos. All of us are linked to the cosmos. . . . So nature is my god. To me, nature is sacred. Trees are my temples and forests are my cathedrals."[1])

But is it not reasonable that the very existence and magnificence of the cosmos is clear evidence that a Creator God wants us to believe and He has been leaving signs of both His power and His love throughout the creation and throughout our life spans?

Reason #2

God wants us to believe because He sees the potential in our lives when we are in a close relationship with Him.

Here is an irony: Sometimes God believes more in us than we believe in ourselves. There is a risk in a generalized statement like this, but here is specifically what I mean: God believes in us not in the sense that we are objects of faith, or even faithful, but in the sense that He sees the potential of our lives—a potential that He Himself put there—and longs for us to draw on all the resources and make the good decisions that will produce a steady path of growth. God wants us to believe in Him because He knows that His power and love are the greatest resources available to us. God believes in what He has done in creating us. Otherwise the Scriptures would not convey the voice of God commanding us forward and cheering us on like a parent knowing just what we are capable of.

I grew up in Green Bay, Wisconsin, not far from Lambeau Field, in the days when Bart Starr, the championship-winning quarterback, led the team under the brilliant coaching of Vince Lombardi. And as my children grew up, they had the thrill of witnessing another history-making quarterback lead the Packers, Brett Favre. I've sat in Lambeau Field many times during the Favre years as tens of thousands of wildly excited fans cheered on the team and its leader—even when the outdoor temperature plunged way below freezing or snow obscured the lines on the field, even when the scoreboard had the Packers losing badly. Whenever Favre completes a great pass, the cheering is strong and personal.

But the cheering on of Brett Favre began many years earlier. There would be no applause in the stadium if there had not been the applause—and rigorous training and correction—of Favre's own live-at-home coach, Irvin Favre, his father.

In the small south Mississippi town of Kiln, Irvin Favre was the coach of the Hancock North High School football team. And it wasn't nepotism but demonstrated talent and developed skill that won Brett the quarterback position on his dad's team. For three years, Brett was the starting quarterback; and despite Brett's excellent throwing arm, Irvin Favre did not showcase his son but executed a predominantly running game, because he judged that to be the best winning strategy. This is how a future three-time NFL Most Valuable Player and Super Bowl-winning quarterback grew up. Loving the game, loving his father/coach. Lovingly cajoled and corrected and cheered by his father—but not used by his father as a trophy. The close connection between them allowed the father's knowledge and wisdom to take his son's potential and turn it into extraordinary heart and skill. And millions of people had the pleasure of watching.

In the Super Bowl of 1997, Brett Favre still looked like a high-school kid having the time of his life, doing fake-out moves that they do in high school but nobody bothers with in the pros. The Super Bowl win was the high point of Irvin Favre's life.

On December 21, 2003, one day before a Monday-night game pitting the Packers against the Oakland Raiders, Brett Favre got a phone call he wasn't expecting. His 58-year-old father was found dead in his pickup truck near the family home in Kiln, tumbled into a ditch, probably after a heart attack. In a moment, the father who came to almost every one of the 204 consecutive games Brett started in was gone. The family unanimously urged Brett to follow through with the Monday-night game, and on that night he played one of the most brilliant games in his career, passing for four touchdowns in the first half and a total of 399 yards in a 41-7 victory. Amazing. Afterward, Favre said, "I knew that my dad would have wanted me to play. I love him so much and I love this game. It's meant a great deal to me, to my dad and to my family. I didn't expect this kind of performance."[2]

Six years earlier, after the Super Bowl win, coach Irvin Favre had said, "It's hard to believe that the little boy we raised has done all this."[3]

God will never say, "This is too hard to believe." God knows what we are capable of—both the wickedness and the goodness. God is never surprised, He never gives up, and He never expects us to perform in life solo. God wants us to believe in Him—as Father, as Coach, as Lord and as Master. God longs for us to believe in Him—not because He is incomplete without us, but because He knows how incomplete we are without Him.

Reason #3

God wants us to believe because it is the only way for us to become what we were created to be: the image and likeness of God.

The potential that God sees in our lives goes far beyond our performing well on the field of life. This is the limitation of the athletic performance analogy. The Bible does say that we should strive toward the finish line in the race of life, and that we should persevere with the endurance that God gives us in life (see 1 Cor. 9:24; Heb. 12:1). But the Bible does not say that God runs the world by looking for the superstars and rewarding them with blessing upon blessing (do any of us think that it would be a good thing if only one in ten thousand of us had the potential to be a real player in God's eyes?). Rather, God bestows on the ordinary person the calling of living as a person created in God's own image. Everyone is ordinary in this sense (we are all created in God's image [see Gen. 1:27]), but that makes us all extraordinary.

To be created in the image and likeness of God means everything. It is our essential identity, so it is the key to understanding life. One person will think that her Norwegian background is her essential identity, another that his profession as a doctor is the essence, another that her skinny frame is her essence. But no such characteristics get down to the core, to the true essence of what makes us us.

In 2003, a massive 13-year scientific endeavor called The Human Genome Project was completed. It was the greatest effort in history to define the essence of humanity by identifying all 20,000 to 25,000 genes in human DNA, determining the sequences of the three billion chemical combinations that make up human DNA and committing all of this to databases so that the science could be applied in further research into disease and treatment, among other applications. If ever there was a scientific endeavor to define humanity (a task requiring the work of hundreds of scientists from 18 different countries), this appeared to be it.

And there was one other goal of the Human Genome Project: to address the ethical, legal and social issues that may arise from the project. What about genetic engineering? What about cloning? This last goal (for which relatively few budgetary dollars were allocated) shows that for all of the fascinating research into the makeup of a human being, we do reach a point where we realize there is more to person-hood than three billion chemical combinations. Personhood exceeds DNA.

How do we know that? How do we know we are not just physical but metaphysical as well? Who says that "the image of God" in Genesis 1:27 is nothing more than a passing poet-ic expression? And what does any of this have to do with the quality of life? Why should we care?

We have to care because any of us, though made in the image of God, can descend to a level of brokenness and destructiveness that is at the root of the problems of every family, every community and the world itself. We can take nuclear material and create nuclear power plants or nuclear bombs, we can build hospitals or torture chambers, we can raise children who become a blessing to almost everyone they influence or who become habitual criminals, and our marriages can be places of safety and healing or sources of our deepest wounds.

But we were designed in the likeness of God. The essence of personhood will never be defined as the combination of DNA determining whether your eyes are blue or your hair blond, whether you are five foot six or six foot one, or whether you're a man or a woman.

My wife treasures old photos of her family members going back four and five generations. The photos are yel-lowed and cracked. The characters in those photos are straight-faced, suit- and corset-bound, joyless, looking like they were still traumatized by their Atlantic crossing or had just eaten something terribly sour. Whenever the box of old photos comes out of the closet, we can't help but sit on the couch and study those faces again. In one of the pictures is a woman named Matilda, who looks like someone who could plant whole fields in Sweden with her bare hands. (I was so glad the day I learned that in those days, people had to make their faces go flat because the photographic exposure was so long that any movement would show up as a blur. Nobody said "Say cheese" in those days.) My wife keeps these images because they are the record of her origins. I looked at some of my family's heirloom photos once; and while I scanned them in disbelief that those people with wildly-shaped hair were my roots, my eye landed on one person whose face—at least the nose, eyes, brow, chin and shape—did actually look like mine. It was shocking, like accidentally seeing your face in a mirror at the end of a very long hallway.

Now, most of us have a hard time believing that we're made in the image of God. And that's probably appropriate, because the image of God in the human race is terribly defaced and tarnished. There are some people who believe that we human beings are little gods, sparks flying off the great fire of divinity. Other people come at life from the opposite extreme, seeing themselves as nothing more than advanced species of animals. But probably most people live between those extremes, knowing that there is some kind of homing instinct in them that keeps them looking for God, wanting to believe. They believe they have spirit and soul. When they hear about the life and teaching of Jesus, there is something arresting in it all—a face that draws you in, like that face in the old photograph that seems like the archetype of who you were always meant to be.

Scripture—arguably the most honest set of writings the world has ever seen—says that humanity was indeed created in God's image but that human history shows how tarnished that image has become. There are at least three ways the Scriptures say we are created to be like God: our creativity, our morality and our spirituality.

However far we have fallen, human beings, like God (but also unlike God), *can create*. We can turn a desert into a thriving community (whether in the fashion of the modern Israelis who irrigated and brought to life vast tracts of desert, or in the fashion of the gangsters who created Las Vegas). We can conceive of buildings that have never been dreamed up or built before and make them real—the Taj Mahal, Frank Lloyd Wright's Fallingwater, the one-room cabin I lived in during my high school summers. We create plays and novels, songs and symphonies, radiology scanning machines and communications technologies. So it may be said that human beings are like God in that we can create, but our creating is on a whole different level from God's. We can invent and design some impressive things, but the most we do is rearrange matter—God brought matter into existence. A creative human artist may paint a still life, the morning light streaming into the studio, illuminating a bowl of fruit on a table. But God is the only Creator who could say, "Let there be light," and who also created the fruit that the artist tries to imitate in his painting.

Another bit of evidence that we are created in the image of God is that *we are moral beings*. That is not to say that we are morally upright all the time or even most of the time. In fact, it is hard to argue that there is any human action that is completely pure in motive and morality. Yet we know we are moral beings because we have this inner sense of "ought" and "ought not." We assume that some things are right and others are not right. We want justice, even if we live in a time and place where hardly anybody shows any sense of justice. True, some people are serial killers or tyrants. Clearly, there are people who have fallen so far from any semblance of morality and decency that they seem to be essentially immoral. Hopelessly lost. But because the wider society can recognize serial killers and recoil at them and put them behind bars when they murder, we have further evidence that morality, or at least a moral sensitivity and longing, is woven into the nature of human beings.

The moral argument for the existence of God says this: The moral longings, aspirations and expectations of human beings have no material explanation and so they suggest a higher being behind it all. Where else could our sense of fairness and justice come from? Why would it matter if someone supported his or her grandmother or stole from her? Why do soldiers throw themselves on live hand grenades in order to save the lives of their buddies?

This argument for the existence of God does not hinge on whether, as you read this, you think of yourself as a fairly moral person or as stuck in a sinkhole of immorality. The very fact of your awareness, or that you would even care, shows that you have a voice in you that comes from a higher place. And that voice is calling you to a higher level of living. It is why you want to believe.

The prodigal son, having wasted the inheritance he prematurely grabbed from his father with one long party, had one thought in his mind as he lived a burnt-out impoverished life: I want to go back home. But why? Is "home" with

God just a more prosperous place to live? Not necessarily. To be "at home" with God is to come back to a place of order—moral order in particular. And we know that is the best place to live.

One morning recently my mother looked out the window in the front of her house just as a car pulled up to the curb and two young men wearing hoods shuffled to the front door of the house next door, leaving the driver in the car, and in a few moments, disappeared inside. My mother knew instinctually that something looked suspicious about it all, and so she got her binoculars and, hands shaking, scribbled down the license number of the car. She was about to call the police when a squad car appeared (another watchful neighbor had placed the call), and a policeman approached the front of the house. Just then the car at the curb sped away and a moment later the guys inside the house burst out the backdoor, scampered across my mother's backyard and into the woods to the back. Mom called me, barely able to speak at first. Seventy-five years old and a widow, she was shaken by the crime unfolding before her eyes. And she was sensitized to it. A few years earlier, she had returned home to find a broken window on the backside of the house facing the woods and evidence that someone had been rummaging through her house.

The sense of violation we feel when our house is broken into or when a corrupt corporate chief steals from shareholders or when a politician is found to have accepted bribes or when a woman is raped in her car goes beyond our fear that our own safety sometime might be compromised. We sense the inherent wrongness in these things. Like spotting cracks in the iron girders of a bridge that could be signs of impending disaster, we know that any compromise of integrity (a word engineers use to describe the soundness and wholeness of a thing) is a threat to everybody. We want elected officials and enforcement officers to apply rules of law and order. And we know that standards of law and order are best when they come to us from the outside—from a higher plane. That's why, at the Supreme Court building in Washington, DC, there is a bas-relief of Moses holding the scroll of the Ten Commandments. We're looking for ultimate laws that protect us from physical harm and robbery, not based on municipal codes that define civil behavior, but based on a voice from heaven that says, "Thou shalt NOT . . ." God wants us to believe because that is our only hope to get real moral clarity and to have a foundation of justice in life that protects us.

A third way that we are made in the image of God is that *we are spiritual creatures.* Human beings can't help relating to God. Sometimes that means searching for God, and other times it means running away from God. But whether you're a person who is bushwhacking his or her way to God—reading, discussing, praying, meditating—or trying to get away from the idea that an all-knowing God is watching your every move, we all show that we are different from the rest of the animal kingdom. Chimpanzees may be trained to communicate, and once in a great while scientists will find an animal that "invents" a new way to crack a nut, but no animal species ever demonstrated religious habits. We will never find in the deep dark woods an altar to worship God that was created by the woodland creatures. You will never descend the stairs in the morning and find your cat or dog reading Scripture and praying. Spirituality is unique to the human race, because humanity was made in God's own image.

God wants us to believe because it is the only way for us to become what we were created to be: the image and likeness of God.

Reason #4

God wants us to believe because God knows about pain.

One of the most helpless feelings I ever get is when I visit someone in the hospital or hospice who is in the midst of a degenerative illness for which there is no cure or who has suffered some kind of bone-crushing accident that will require months of recovery, with no guarantee of quality of life afterward.

Mary was a good friend to me and my wife. Bright-eyed and likely to laugh at every possible opportunity, she attracted good-spirited people to herself, typically resulting in uproariously pleasurable dinners and board games. She had two beautiful young girls whom she and her husband cherished. She did the hard work of doing professional counseling and helped people get a sense of hope back in their lives.

But just when Mary was as vigorous and full of life as can be, she discovered a lump and found herself thrust into the medical system—biopsy, further exploratory surgery, mastectomy. Had the cancer spread to the lymphatic system? Yes, it had. Several nodes affected and removed. Radiation and chemo quickly followed.

Mary knew what it all added up to. Wearing a scarf or a wig was tolerable. She easily turned that into a joke. Extreme fatigue and the inability to take care of her kids were deeply distressing. The prognosis measured time in months at the very most.

Mary believed in God, and she had no inclination to run from God at this time but to cling more closely than ever before. She welcomed the prayers of friends, even if the prayers were awkward, halting and given through choked throats. This was the wrestling time. And she wrestled, well . . . right up to the time of her passing.

What I have seen so many times in people like Mary is that they take comfort from God, not only because of God's strength, but also because of God's own suffering. It is a mystery for sure, but the story of Jesus begins: "In the beginning was the Word, and the Word was with God, and the Word was God . . . and the Word became flesh" (John 1:1-14); and the story ends with the Word who is God having spikes driven through His hands and feet and then being hoisted up in the air on a cross that was slammed into the socket that held it upright, the unsupported body not being able to draw in full breaths, the sun baking the quickly drying exposed skin—and all the rest: the taunting, the humiliation, the mockery. Beauty effaced. The Lord of life put to death.

To many people, pain is the most significant argument against the existence of God (or, at least, a good God). But through the voices of dozens of prophets and apostles and Jesus Himself in the Scriptures, the message is this: God wants you to believe because God does, in fact, know pain, not as a spectator, but as a sufferer. In fact, if all human beings are the offspring of God, then God suffers as a parent to see any pain.

And that leads to an obvious question: Why doesn't God put a stop to it? The Scriptures say that He can and one day He will. At some point yet to come, God will blow the whistle, bring this game to an end and then remake the whole thing—the creation of a new heaven and a new earth.

One day I met with a doctor who was visiting the U.S. from China. He wanted to ask me about faith because he found himself—though he had grown up with an absolutely atheistic worldview—strangely attracted to belief in God. But he had a tough question. Why would a good God bring more and more people into a world that has so much suffering in it? He put it on the table. The big question. The moral dilemma. And I knew how I would respond . . . but just before I did, my eye glanced past his shoulder at the two framed photos of my children that I had on the shelf behind him. I asked him to turn around and look at the pictures. And then I told him that though I may not have words that would completely satisfy his honest question (a question I respected), I did know this: My wife and I know about the good things in life and the sufferings. We've experienced both in life. But for all that, we valued our own lives and wanted to have children. Not for selfish reasons, but because the gift of life is so great, and the good things in life are so much more substantial than the hard times, that we believed it a good thing to bring another human life or two into the world.

Pain can and does sometimes drive people to the point of despairing of life. But most of the time, people find from unexpected sources ways to endure, and find comfort, and even healing. And in the meantime, God has prepared a place on the other side of the hospice bed and the crumpled car. And that is one more reason to believe.

Reason #5

God wants us to believe so that we are moving toward Him
when we die, not running away from Him.

There will be more on the question of life after death in a later chapter, but suffice it to say for now that the issue of eternal destiny, as Jesus talked about it, is always a matter of direction: We choose to move toward God (and so God says to us, "I'm glad you want to be home. Welcome!"), or we choose to ignore God or run away from Him (and so God says, "It's your choice. I'm not going to impose Myself on you now, and I won't for eternity either"). Common sense would tell us that good people with a pile of merits will be rewarded with blessing in the afterlife—call it heaven, paradise, being with God. And common sense would say that if there is anything like hell, it is reserved for the most wicked, blood-thirsty tyrants.

But this is like thinking about God as a boss who will give you a bonus for work well done or as a cop who will toss you in jail and throw away the key if your behavior is antisocial.

This surely misses the point. If we're asking the question, *Why would God want us to believe?* then we have to accurately think about who that God is. If God is "our Father in heaven" (Matt. 6:9) and "my shepherd" (Gen. 48:15; Ps. 23:1) and "my refuge and my fortress" (Ps. 91:2) and "my deliver-er," (2 Sam. 22:2; Pss. 18:2; 40:17; 70:5; 144:2), then it is clear that in this life and in the life to come, the only question is whether we will choose to believe that and live now in the mode of running to God every day and running away from our selfishness, indulgence and corruption—or not.

And the question of what happens to us after we die becomes a direct extension of what we have been doing while we live. If we come to the place of believing that *God* wants us to believe, instead of focusing on the issue of whether we feel like we have enough reasons to believe, then we will come not just to a Power, but also to a Father. Or as it says in one place in the New Testament:

> You have not come to a physical mountain, to a place of flaming fire, darkness, gloom, and whirlwind, as the Israelites did at Mount Sinai when God gave them his laws. For they heard an awesome trumpet blast and a voice with a message so terrible that they begged God to stop speaking. . . .
>
> No, you have come to Mount Zion, to the city of the living God, the heavenly Jerusalem, and to thousands of angels in joyful assembly. You have come to the assembly of God's firstborn children, whose names are written in heaven. You have come to God himself, who is the judge over all people. And you have come to the spirits of the redeemed in heaven who have now been made perfect. You have come to Jesus, the one who mediates the new covenant between God and people, and to the sprinkled blood, which graciously forgives instead of crying out for vengeance as the blood of Abel did (Heb. 12:18-24, *NLT*).

God wants us to believe, not so that we will be polite and well mannered, not because He is looking for slaves to perform arbitrary tasks, and not even so that the world will be a better place. God wants us to believe because He wants *us*.

Notes

1. Mikhail Gorbachev, quoted in Fred Matser, "Nature Is My God," *Resurgence* magazine online. http://www.resurgence.org/resurgence/184/gorbachev.htm (accessed June 2007).
2. "NFL News: Favre, Parish, Cundiff Earn NFC Awards," *NFL.com,* December 24, 2003.
3. Thomas Content, "Families Proud of Dads, Sons," Green Bay *Press-Gazette,* January 1997.

CHAPTER 3

Eternity in Our Hearts

In the Sawi villages in the jungles of Irian Jaya, New Guinea, the way you become a "legend maker" is by pretending to be someone's friend, drawing him in, making him trust you—and then killing him. There is a native phrase for it, roughly translated as "to fatten with friendship for unexpected slaughter."

For generations, this head-hunting and cannibalistic tribe had lived in continual warfare with other villages. Missionary Don Richardson went to live among them, learned their language and tried to bring them a message about God and Jesus, but none of it made sense to them. Richardson was about to leave because his presence seemed only to bring the villages into closer contact and produce more conflict; but the warriors were distressed at the prospect of losing their source of modern medicine and steel axes, so they pledged they would seek peace with each other. *But what kind of peace is really possible here?* Richardson wondered. What he learned was astonishing.

In Sawi culture the one way to guarantee peace between villages is an exchange of infants. A *tarop tim,* or "peace child," is a guarantee of peace, as long as the child is alive. Richardson explained to the tribe that this is what God has done for the human race. The Son of God, Jesus Christ, came as a peace child to put an end to our enmity, our treachery and our blood thirst. Many of the Sawi were transformed by the message, and the warring between villages tapered off.[1]

Stories abound of bits and pieces of spiritual truth lying like seeds in cultures all over the world, evidence that we want to believe because God has put something in our hearts and in our cultures just waiting to sprout and pop up out of the ground one day. Richardson calls them "redemptive analogies." C. S. Lewis called it an echo resounding through all history and culture. G. K. Chesterton wrote about it in his book *Everlasting Man*.

There is a remarkable statement in the book of Ecclesiastes in the Old Testament: "He [God] has made everything beautiful in its time. He has also set eternity in the human heart" (Eccles. 3:11, *TNIV*). Though we are made creatures—breathing, eating, sleeping, reproducing bodies along with the rest of the mammals—we also have this characteristic that keeps us looking to the spiritual side of life. God has "set eternity in the human heart." That is why we want to believe.

If we were only physical beings, then we'd simply carry on living like animals. If we were only spiritual beings, then we'd live like angels. (But few think that.)

What is made and what is eternal—two worlds, but not a contradiction and not a separation, because what is Made came from the Eternal. Most people who believe in God understand God to be the Creator. So God, the eternal one, made my body, the trees from which were cut the lumber that became my house, the grains from which my breakfast cereal comes, and even the silicon from which a Japanese company manufactured the screen for my television.

God made my children. In comparison to God, my wife
and I were not much more than spectators. Yes, we did want
to have children, and my wife needed surgery to make it possible to clear up endometriosis in order to conceive, and we
did do the classes and turned a bedroom upstairs into a
nursery. All very impressive. Ingrid prepared the house carefully for the big transition, and on the morning she woke up
with contractions, I dutifully drove her to the hospital just
fast enough to get there quickly but not so fast as to get
pulled over for speeding. Although in the back of my mind
was this imagined dramatic moment: I'd drive as fast as I
wanted. If pulled over, I'd shout at the cop, "My wife is in
labor!" and he'd turn his blue and red lights and siren on
and become an escort for the three most important people
on the planet at that moment. Didn't happen. I drove the
speed limit, and just a bit more. But I must have been day-
dreaming because I drove right past the correct freeway exit.
I hoped Ingrid, who appeared to be dozing quietly but was
actually practicing relaxation exercises, wouldn't notice my
slow deceleration and oh-so-delicate U-turn. Not a chance.
One eye slightly opened. "You missed the exit?" was all she
needed to say—so slowly, so incredulously. That wouldn't
have been so bad if I hadn't turned the wrong way when we
left the driveway back home. And that wouldn't have been so
bad if I hadn't forgotten the suitcase in the house. And that
wouldn't have been so bad if I hadn't given the nurse in the
emergency room (once we got to the hospital) totally random numbers when she asked me for my wife's height and
weight. I didn't know the numbers, I didn't care, and I
resented a person with a clipboard asking such ridiculous
things when my wife (who sat in a wheelchair with her eyes

closed again) was going to go through this most remarkable thing. Again, one eye slightly opened. Apparently, I had made her five inches taller and 20 pounds heavier than she actually was. Bad move.

Yes, we did all that. We were so impressive as expectant parents. But, truth be told, we were basically spectators. God did this thing. I don't know how to make an arm. I didn't construct the baby's heart. I didn't wire the brain or organize the genetics stored on every chromosome. And I know I didn't fashion a soul. Once again a new human being was made by Eternity and *for* eternity. And when the hospital wheeled my wife down to the exit and I strapped the baby carefully in the back seat of our small four-door and drove away, I thought, *Now what do we do?*

I've got a great admiration for people who create things. I've had just a taste of what it is to build an outdoor addition to our house, to sit on a committee with architects who designed a multimillion-dollar project, to make things out of clay on the potter's wheel, to print a photo in the darkroom, or to make music at the keyboard. Other people I've met are far better makers. I'm impressed with what they can make, like my engineer friend Keith who was on the team that designed the rocket boosters of the Saturn V that took men to the moon and back, and like the man I met who was one of the workers who chiseled granite with dynamite to make four faces on a mountain in South Dakota. But the thing about home additions and rockets and Mt. Rushmore is that we human beings are just rearranging molecules. We don't really *make* anything.

Our best chance for living good days and having some quality of life is having our eyes wide open to these two worlds: the Made and the Eternal. Why does it matter? The Eternal dignifies the Made. It defines its purpose. It warns me about my limitations. God the eternal inhabits the Creation He made. Believing in God lets me know that my bank account is not the measure of my worth. Believing is the way I know I'm more than an animal. Believing connects me with another world where all is right and just and harmonious— a world that can impress itself on the Made world like a die stamped on soft metal. Believing in God assures me that my happiness 20 years from now is not really going to be based on the size of my bank account at that time. Believing tempers my passions and leads me away from temptations and delivers me from evil.

No wonder I want to believe.

So the writer of Ecclesiastes puts forth this proposition: "God has made everything beautiful in its time. He has also set eternity in the human heart." Then the writer goes on to say:

> Yet no one can fathom what God has done from beginning to end. I know that there is nothing better for people than to be happy and to do good while they live. That each of them may eat and drink, and find satisfaction in all their toil—this is the gift of God. I know that everything God does will endure forever; nothing can be added to it and nothing taken from it. God does it so that people will fear him (Eccles. 3:11-14, *TNIV*).

The person who wrote this must have been dreading going in to work that day. Why else would he call it "toil"?

Why else would he be searching for God to give some appropriate meaning to going out to dusty fields or whatever his labor was going to be that day? This is also a person who really enjoys eating and drinking and finding satisfaction. He is not afraid to imagine the Eternal intersecting the Made.

The writer talks about eating and drinking and having satisfaction—but don't think he's a hedonist. It isn't just about the food. He wants his mealtimes to have meaning. He wants his toil to have meaning. He wants to believe. And he does believe that the satisfaction of the body today is connected with the eternal world if he sees his dinner and every other appropriate physical satisfaction as "the gift of God."

It may not seem like a big deal. Sure, thank God for supper. Pray, "Give us this day our daily bread," and then chow down. But it is a huge deal. Believing, really believing (because we really do want to believe this), that our lives are full of very ordinary almost unnoticeable movements that, on closer examination, are a thousand gifts of God changes the ordinary into the extraordinary. A meal is a gift, a day of work is a gift, a good conversation is a gift. A car is a gift, an hour of worship is a gift, a day at the ballpark with your kid is a gift, narrowly avoiding an auto accident is a gift. If this did nothing more than fill us with gratitude every day, our lives would be revolutionized. Gratitude sees gifting in the most ordinary events: a night out with your spouse, an article in the newspaper that tells the truth, a verse of Scripture that bounces around in your head, an hour of quiet.

Gratitude will change your life, but this is about more than gratitude. Seeing the Eternal behind the Made, and seeing yourself as a creature that can perceive both, makes you stop and look at everything differently. As C. S. Lewis once said, "I believe in Christianity as I believe that the sun has risen—not only because I see it, but because by it I see everything else."[2]

If your spouse is Made, then you have to treat him or her with respect. If your body is Made, then you must not hurt it with excessive drinking or drugs, because you'd be desecrating a temple God made for His purposes. If this world is Made, then you have to believe that turning the atmosphere or water supply into poison is an insult to God. He started with a garden; we should not turn it into a wasteland. If your children are Made, then the whole point in raising them is not coercion, control and complaining about the cost they are to you. Child-rearing is an effort to bring into society a human being who will improve it, and to bring another eternal being into the kingdom of God.

The writer of Ecclesiastes precedes what he has to say about God's making everything beautiful, and putting eternity in our hearts, with this memorable statement:

> There is a time for everything, and a season for every
> activity under the heavens:
>   a time to be born and a time to die,
>   a time to plant and a time to uproot,
>   a time to kill and a time to heal,
>   a time to tear down and a time to build,
>   a time to weep and a time to laugh,
>   a time to mourn and a time to dance,
>   a time to scatter stones and a time to gather them,
>   a time to embrace and a time to refrain,
>   a time to search and a time to give up,
>   a time to keep and a time to throw away,

a time to tear and a time to mend,
a time to be silent and a time to speak,
a time to love and a time to hate,
a time for war and a time for peace (Eccles. 3:1-8).

This passage is about the seasonality of life. We go through seasons in life, so we don't need to be despondent; on the other hand, we shouldn't take good times for granted. War will give way to peace. Mourning will give way to dancing, tearing down will be followed by times of building. We've got to take a wider view of life.

So much of life is about timing. Speaking up and staying silent are both fine, but when we jabber on when we should shut up or clam up when we should open up—those are instances of the right thing at the wrong time. Some days you should gather; other days it's better to toss. But if you spend money on stuff when you really can't afford to or divest yourself when you should be conserving, you may be doing a perfectly appropriate thing at the wrong time. Managing the Made is one of the great challenges in life. Our best hope is that the values of the Eternal tell us how to manage the Made.

You can take it from there. Go ahead and fill in your life circumstances. A time to go to college and a time to graduate. A time to be healthy and a time to be ill. A time to save your money and a time to invest it. A time to make decisions for your kids and a time to let them make their own decisions. A time to live in the city and a time to live in the country. A time to pray with other people and a time to pray alone. A time to compliment and a time to complain. A time to say you're sorry and a time to tell someone else he or she should be sorry. We make life-altering decisions as frequently and as fast as driving a hundred miles an hour down the road.

"God has set eternity in the human heart" explains why each of us carries through the day this longing to believe that we can behave better than animals and make decisions that will lead to good things. But this truth also has a wider, universal meaning for the whole human race.

Throughout the modern era, everyone who has studied movements in the human race—anthropologists, sociologists, psychologists, biologists, historians, philosophers, theologians—has wanted to explain why certain "eternal" themes come up in virtually every culture. We know of the origins and development of the major world religions, of course. Christianity, Judaism, Islam, Buddhism, Hinduism have adherents that number in the hundreds of millions. But there are thousands of smaller stories of people encountering God in dreams, in nature and in long-standing legends. Why does God keep appearing almost everywhere the human race looks?

One of my professors in college gave us one of the stock scholarly explanations for religiosity and the widespread belief in God in the human race. *It's all about fear,* he said. Every species of animal has a sense of self-preservation. Every animal will flee or fight if threatened. But human beings, with their advanced brain development, calm their fears (particularly, the fear of death) by a cognitive leap, a belief that some greater being is able to rescue them from death. But it is still about the nerve mass we call the brain coming up with ways of avoiding neurological pain in the extremities. It is the caveman running away from the bear and thinking that maybe there's a shelter better than a tree he can shimmy up. One such creature thought one day, *Let us pray*.

That, in this professor's opinion, is why we want to believe.

It is all about recoiling from physical threat, all about preservation of the body. Human beings, as really advanced animals, add this to running or fighting: They can dream. Their brain chemistry has a more pleasant effect when endorphins are flowing, so they invent a fantasy of a greater being who can protect them. The idea of "God" or "gods" offers more endorphins than the tree or cave.

The implication of all this is that penguins and deer and shrews are fundamentally more honest than human beings. Eat or be eaten—that's their agenda, and there is no clouding of the issue of life and death with dreams about a God who isn't actually there.

Now there are some people who boldly say that we're animals with bigger brains that sometimes lead us into fantasy, but we'd do better to just get over it and be content to be the eating, drinking, working, reproducing, dying creatures that we are and leave it at that. Some people who hold that view are very bright and hold advanced degrees. They have no problem saying that human beings have invented or imagined the idea of God. But we have to notice this: There are far more people who still want to believe—even though they think they may be taking a risk. And they're not just looking for an updated myth. They seem to naturally conceive of a Being that is greater than all others, and they believe that the supreme Being that almost everything points to *really exists*. Ultimate greatness implies real existence. (Philosophers call this the ontological proof for the existence of God.)

It's hard to give up dignity—and that is, of course, what you are doing if you conclude that we are nothing more than animals. It's hard to convince yourself that the visions of God that fill the world are just mass delusions. If practically the whole human race is wrong about something like that, then what is the human race right about?

But the evidence for believing is broad and overwhelming. It isn't just that there are billions of people in the world who hold to some kind of belief in God or gods. There are specific things about God that are held in common by many of the major religions and are also discovered in hidden tribes.

One of those common themes is salvation through the dying god. Much of the world's great literature springs from the streams of mythologies that get passed around like a kind of family history. And it has been pointed out many times that the frequency with which "the dying god" appears in mythologies from different times and places suggests that this idea moves like a meandering stream through numerous cultures.

But what if it is a story (in all its various forms) based on a great truth, like a brook issuing from a subterranean, hidden source—a spring of life-giving water for the thirsty human race? What if the human family keeps coming up with this idea—that a divine being has to come, that he will speak eternal truth and that life will come through his death—because it's true? Then the gospel message—that God came into the world to save the world, that He did this at a specific time and in a specific place, that Jesus, whose family came from Nazareth, was this being who is a real person and divine as well, and who died and rose from death—is true. It cannot be denied that over the past 2,000 years, hundreds of millions of people have believed that this vision has become fact: The Creator God sends a savior who dies and then takes life back, sending a wave of healing and life-restoring energy into the human race.

An ever-widening swath of the human race has come to believe that because it wants to believe it. But it is not a wanting that makes things up or latches onto a fantasy as a kind of spiritual painkiller. It is a wanting that is a predisposition of thought and emotion and action coming from a truth so conspicuous and so loud that it echoes throughout the human race. This is that shout: The Creator God who "made everything beautiful" and who "set eternity in the human heart" couldn't possibly leave us alone with the errors and crimes we commit. He must be good, He must help us, and He must help in the only life-saving way He can. This is the Eternity that is stuck in our hearts.

I came to believe this one day when I was cutting vegetables in the dark back storage room of my grandfather's general store.

Wills' General Store in Ellison Bay, Wisconsin, was a white-block single-story boxy building that had just six aisles or so but where you could find any canned fruit, bandages, popular magazines, good cuts of meat and fresh vegetables you could want. It was the non-superstore, where there were 6 of any given item, not 200. I worked in the dark back room where boxes of inventory were piled to the ceiling.

I was 17 years old. I was doing that monotonous kind of job that you do over and over again but which allows your mind to wander and probe, not really knowing where it will end up. This was a bit risky because it was August and a few 50-pound boxes of sweet corn had some into the storage room and I had to take each ear, hold it out in front of me, chop off the end with a very sharp 12-inch knife, flip it around in the air and then chop off the other end. I got used to doing it every day very fast, so the shocks and the stocks were flying. In the rhythmic concentration, I was thinking about what I had been reading in the Bible—specifically, the life and teaching of Jesus in the Gospel of John.

And that was when it hit me (and I wasn't expecting to get "hit" by anything in my mind). It just hit me that the story I had heard from the time I was in Sunday School really did fit into everything obvious about the created world and the broken, conflicted, disgusting, amazing human race. *It just fits,* I thought, *that a God who created such a fantastic universe would do whatever He could to fix what was broken, even if He wasn't the one who broke it. I'd do that, after all, if I were a father and I saw my children suffering the consequences of their own mistakes. And it fits that God would do this in person because there really wasn't any other way to do it. And it fits that Jesus of Nazareth—who was human enough to be the son of Mary and a man who wept at His best friend's tomb but who also did divine things like forgiving people their sins and letting people worship Him and healing people and calming storms—would be exactly the Savior that the world would need and God would send.*

Now I know that people like the pastors and Sunday School teachers I grew up under faithfully told me the story I needed to know and understand. But there's a difference between hearing and understanding. You can know the details of the story but not know the story. Seeing the pieces is not like seeing the whole. It is like the difference between dating, courtship and exchanging vows. When someone first gets to know the man or woman whom he or she will marry, it begins with a fact-gathering mission. You are intrigued, interested and maybe even infatuated. But early on, you are just gathering the bits and pieces—favorite foods, favorite musician, greatest fear, opinion of parents' marriage. So many details, so many facts. But then there comes a point when you believe you have crossed the line of knowing. A person has emerged in this exploration, a person you'd like to spend your life with. A person who is your soul mate.

Many of us heard the story of Jesus Christ, even learned all the details, but there needed to be a time and place when it all came together—and then we really did believe. It's just a little like the day you came to believe you could trust a person—really trust him or her—as the love of your life. After a considerable amount of time gathering bits and pieces of evidence that this other person loves you and you are inclined to love in return, you take the plunge.

I take no credit in coming to understand the story of Jesus Christ and coming to really believe. It wasn't that I got especially bright or that I deciphered a riddle that takes the mind of a Sherlock Holmes. It's not that I decided to seek a purer heart or turn my life over to God. It's not that I took the time to read a dozen books on theology. I was just cutting corn—but the big ideas of Scripture fell into place for me just like when you can see a jigsaw puzzle solution and your fingers can't move fast enough to get the remaining pieces in place.

And, of course, that day when the pieces came together in my mind was not really the entire experience of coming to believe. It was just one step, preceded by a walk I had started earlier that summer when I started to read the New Testament for myself. Actually, the walk started much earlier, with steps so small during my growing-up years that they were long-ago forgotten.

I'm glad I don't need to understand exactly what happened on that day and on all the days previous and since, as I took the steps of believing. I could spend a lot of time analyzing it all, but that would only lead me to think that this is all about me. But it is not about me. Believing is not mainly about the believer. It is about what is believed—or to put it better, it is about the eternal reality that inspires the belief. Believing is what happens when, in our consciousness, two worlds are conjoined: the Made and the Eternal. And then what we see before our eyes and our hands can touch merges with the mysterious and the supernatural. We gain our first truly comprehensive view of life.

This is the reason why the Bible says God, who is spirit, is like the wind that comes from one direction and then another—invisibly, powerfully, effectively. You don't make the wind blow, and you can't even predict it. But the same wind that gave breath to the man and the woman at the creation is the God who gives life to us now.

Earlier this year I got one of those late-night calls that makes you jump and start to wonder even before you get to the phone and lift the receiver to your ear. It was a pastor colleague.

"Just wanted to let you know that Frank Nelson had a major heart attack earlier this evening and passed away at Waukesha Memorial just within the last half hour."

I had known Professor Frank Nelson since I was a college student. He taught the history of education at the University of Wisconsin and was known as a stickler of a teacher, probing his students with penetrating questions in the Socratic style. He was tall and large with a hefty shock of white hair. That and his resonant voice made his presence all the more imposing. He emigrated from Norway as a boy and kept his Norwegian heritage very close to the surface—chatting enthusiastically with my Scandinavian wife about the old country whenever the opportunity came along.

But more than all that, what I will always remember about Frank Nelson is his deeply formed Christian character. His convictions were strong and as detailed as could be (and if he wanted to press a point, he'd press it with the force of a bulldozer), but he had the kindest, sweetest demeanor when looking a hurting person straight in the eye. He received the standard prayer request lists that get passed around in church, and he absorbed it all. He followed up. He wanted to know what happened with that difficult situation that appeared on the list a month ago.

His wife of 49 years, Lois, was at the side of the gurney in the emergency room when I arrived there. She was sad but calm. The first words out of her mouth when she saw me were simply, "Graduated to glory."

I thought, *What better thing could you say right now?* The big man was prone on the gurney. You would think he was just having a restful night's sleep. Except the breath was gone. God had given him first breath 80 years earlier, and last breath was tonight. He had crossed the line from the Made to the Eternal. Graduation day.

Notes

1. Don Richardson, *Peace Child* (Ventura, CA: Regal Books, 2005).
2. C. S. Lewis, *They Asked for a Paper* (London: Geoffrey Bles, 1962), p. 211.

CHAPTER 4

Whom Should I Believe?

When I was a kid and there was some kind of heated disagreement between me and my friends, the whole argument sometimes boiled down to this refined philosophical query: "Says *who*?"

Now to say it right, you've got to put a lot of *oomph* into the "who." And there has to be an edge of defiance and skepticism in how you say it. So if one guy said, "You can't do that" or "You can't go there" or "You have to do this," and the thing that leapt out of your mouth was "Says *who*?" you were drawing a line in the sand, digging your heels in, staking your territory, standing your ground.

Behind this little exchange, however, is a looming life issue that every person wrestles with: the age-old question of authority. Under what circumstances and from what source will I accept a definitive influence that may affect my actions? And the truth of the matter is this: Most of us want an authoritative word that rings clear and sharp, but we recoil at authority that impinges on our prerogatives or our intended actions. We want it both ways. We want to find truth, but we want to decide whether or not we do anything about it. This then becomes one of our biggest barriers to belief, because "the truth will set you free" (John 8:32), but (if it really is true) it will also hem you in. The freedom that

faith brings means that we break out into reality, but also
that we leave behind anything we find that is false. And we
do so willingly.

Now when it comes to finding truth, there's always a
"who" involved. Finding truth means finding the personal
God who then takes you on a guided tour of a world of
truth. We grasp reality—who we are, what is going on in the
world, who God is, what God intends to do—by listening to
authoritative voices that can be trusted because they are way
out ahead of us. They see down the path. Or they can see
things we cannot. Sometimes our tour guides for life are
trusted friends, spiritual leaders, parents. But we all know,
deep in our hearts, that we need to find the authority of the
Almighty. And we don't know until we find it whether we
will run with abandon to come under God's strength and
protection or whether we'll hesitate, stand at a distance and
slowly step backward.

I can't ever remember being a kid, looking at my mother
and responding, "Says *who*?" I can't say it didn't cross my
mind, and I suppose those two words could easily have
slipped out, but I knew that if I ever did say them, the answer
would be swift and decisive and maybe even apocalyptic:
"Says ME!" And that would be that. Or worse, her response
might be, "*What* did you just say?" (As a parent, I have found
this to be one of the most effective comebacks when one of
my kids lets a careless word of defiance jump out of his or
her mouth.)

I certainly would never have said "Says *who*?" to one of
my teachers. Not just because the teacher would have a pretty swift answer, which would involve a walk to the principal's
office, but also because he or she would pick up the phone

and drag my mother into it and, in my mother's mind, a teacher would have to be an axe-murderer to be called into question. My friend Dennis had parents who always took his side against the teachers, and Dennis always laughed about it with us. Those of us who spent time in the principal's office were jealous of him. He had the best parents in the world, we thought. But later I was glad that my mother believed in and taught me about authority, because none of us knew at that time that we were all headed toward the cynical Vietnam war era when lots of people just gave up on trusting anybody. And I didn't know at the time that my view of authority would shape my whole relationship with my Creator. Thanks to my mother, I was taught that authority is a good and safe thing, even if at times you didn't know who you could trust in Washington.

While I may not say "Says *who?*" on the outside (because of social convention and simple politeness), I have to admit that I say it on the inside all the time. And it's not always a bad thing.

If you take away the edge of defiance and the acid of cynicism, then "Says who?" becomes a perfectly legitimate question when we are evaluating competing authorities. Isn't this the reason why so many of us find stories of law and order so fascinating? Maturing as a human being has to include an ever-sharpening sense of discernment. We have to ask the question "Says who?"—and we'd better find some pretty good answers, otherwise our lives will be unduly shaped by the sophisticated campaigns of advertisers, marketers, pundits, cultists and the next bestseller. If we become older but no wiser, it may be because we have missed opportunities to get better and better at distinguishing truth from error.

Sexual intercourse should be reserved for the marriage covenant. Says who?

It is okay to play the lottery. Says who?

Earth is at risk because of global warming. Says who?

There is more wickedness in the human race than ever before in history. Says who?

Abortion is the taking of a human life. Says who?

It is ethically acceptable for scientists to experiment with human cloning. Says who?

The Green Bay Packers are the greatest team in NFL history. Says who?

Rock music comes from the devil. Says who?

Cremation is an acceptable form of burial. Says who?

Jesus Christ will return one day. Says who?

Believers should not be involved in politics. Says who?

Divorce hurts kids. Says who?

The Chicago Cubs cannot win a World Series because a curse lingers over them. Says who?

There is one God, existing in three Persons. Says who?

Max Weber, the father of modern sociology who wrote in the early twentieth century, knew that authority was one of the most influential dynamics in how societies work. Individuals, groups, organizations and bureaucracies are all-powerful influences that exercise overt and covert influences on us. We may be saying "Says who?" on the inside, but all the while we are consciously or unconsciously being shaped by these forces.

Weber came up with three categories of authority (detailed in several of his books, including *The Three Types of Legitimate Rule*). *Traditional authority* is when the customs, culture, habits and lifestyle of a group we count ourselves part of define what is right and wrong and keep us holding to long-standing patterns of thought and behavior because they are, well, traditional. Things have worked this way in the past, so they should do the same today. This is the sanctity of the tradition. Says *who*? Says the tradition. This is the way we've always done things. (Patently untrue, of course. Nothing has ever been done the same way for all time.)

Legal authority is when the boundaries of what we are allowed to do are defined by norms of rationality as set out in legal codes and (especially in the modern industrialized era) in bureaucracy. Legal codes and bureaucracy are different depending on what society you live in—in American society, we generally look to our courts to apply justice. We're somewhat less assured by the products of bureaucracies because anybody who has had to deal with a bureaucracy knows that they often make what they claim they can accomplish far more difficult and complicated than necessary. But they have authority because we often have no choice but to work within them. We all have to stand in line at the Department of Motor Vehicles, we all have to pay our taxes, we all have to respond when called up for jury duty, we all have to stay in our lanes on the road (unless you move to Italy), and we all have to fill out forms on clipboards at the hospital emergency room before a doctor will see us, unless we're cold unconscious or a leg has been cut off and blood is spurting from an artery.

And then, Weber said, there is *charismatic authority*, perhaps the most interesting of the three types, in which individuals hold sway over others by a personal power and persuasion that goes beyond the rational. Religious authority, not surprisingly, often springs from the charismatic authority exercised by highly visible individuals or the leader of a movement.

Now, as a secularist, Weber naturally assumed that all the major religions of the world, and plenty of smaller ones, have sprung up as a reaction to the charismatic power of some human leader. Whether it is Moses or Jesus or Muhammad or Buddha you're looking at, you understand the movement in the shape of the personality and idiosyncrasies of the founder. Moses, Jesus, Muhammad and Buddha would have disagreed with Weber, claiming that their authority was not simply the extension of their personal charisma, but was derived—that they were the messengers of a truth beyond themselves. Moses was the prophet of Yahweh, Jesus of God the Father, Muhammad of Allah, Buddha of the universe.

Jesus, at this point, is a special case because while He often pointed to the authority of the Father in heaven, He also claimed to be, in His own person, the foundation of faith. The others said, "You should believe in God" or "You should believe in this truth." Jesus added, "You should believe in *Me*."

The Sea of Galilee is a 13-mile-long, heart-shaped lake—fresh and wild and deliciously blue. In the fishing villages around that lake, Jesus gathered followers from all walks of life. And He gave His most memorable speech one day on the northeastern slopes running up from the lake. We know it as the Sermon on the Mount (see Matt. 5–7). Quite a crowd had gathered on that particular day. Rumors of miracles and healings were naturally attracting dozens and then hundreds and eventually thousands of people. At first, they were just Galileans, but then people from Jerusalem in the south, Syria in the north and even people from beyond the Jordan River in the east were mingled in the crowds.

So the slope of the rolling hills became an outdoor amphitheater. People strained to hear what Jesus was saying, those on the fringes having to have His words repeated by those sitting closer. All these centuries later, the words of the Sermon on the Mount still have the ring of truth to them, a compelling and captivating allure. The words arrest our attention. They turn our minds upside down. They stick like burrs, but they also soothe like salve.

"Blessed are those who mourn, for they will be comforted" (5:4).

"You are the salt of the earth" (5:13).

"Love your enemies" (5:44).

"When you give to the needy, do not let your left hand know what your right hand is doing" (6:3).

"Do not store up for yourselves treasures on earth, where moth and rust destroy, and where thieves break in and steal. But store up for yourselves treasures in heaven" (6:19-20).

"You cannot serve both God and Money" (6:24).

"Who of you by worrying can add a single hour to his life?" (6:27).

"Do not judge, or you too will be judged" (7:1).

"Enter through the narrow gate" (7:13).

To say that such words have been memorable and influential would be a great understatement. The teachings of Jesus have shaped history and given definition to civilization. In the final section of Matthew's rendering of the Sermon on the Mount, Jesus teaches about His own teaching:

Everyone who hears these words of mine and puts them into practice is like a wise man who built his house on the rock. The rain came down, the streams rose, and the winds blew and beat against that house; yet it did not fall, because it had its foundation on the rock. But everyone who hears these words of mine and does not put them into practice is like a foolish man who built his house on sand. The rain came down, the streams rose, and the winds blew and beat against that house, and it fell with a great crash (7:24-27).

This is a bold claim. To some, it is an audacious claim. A statement that might prompt a "Says *who*?"

Matthew has this concluding editorial remark: "When Jesus finished saying these things, the crowds were amazed at his teaching, because he taught as one who had authority, and not as their teachers of the law" (7:28-29).

It is not that Jesus appealed to traditional authority. The traditionalists were his enemies. The "teachers of the law" taught differently because all they did was regurgitate tradition (and, particularly, a tradition they had fabricated to elevate their class and protect their prerogatives). It is not that Jesus was wielding legal authority. He held no credentials and His extraordinary influence would increasingly put Him in the category of outlaw. So was it charismatic authority that Jesus possessed? Were the crowds mesmerized by His eyes and His voice? Not really. None of the Gospels say anything about the style of Jesus' speech or His personal bearing. It was apparently *what* He said that grabbed people, not how He said it. One has to believe that as His extraordinary words came out of His mouth, their meaning struck everyone as so beyond-the-ordinary, so unexpected and so conspicuously true that they landed like arrows that sank deep without wounding—or at least they wounded those parts that deserve wounding. People were amazed at His teachings because they were a fireworks of insight that lit up the landscape of their lives. His teachings made them remember: *We want to believe.* And even when they went away mystified or ruffled, they knew they wouldn't be able to forget His words. It became increasingly obvious why the voice of the Father from heaven at the baptism of Jesus said, "This is my Son. . . . Listen to him!" (Mark 9:7).

It is not just that the crowds perceived authority purely divine, but buried in Jesus' words about His own words are these signals, too: *He rewrote the Word of God.*

In the Sermon on the Mount (Matthew 5, specifically), Jesus used the following formula five different times: "You have heard that it was said . . . but I tell you." In each instance, "what was said" is a quote from the Old Testament Law—God's Word given at Mt. Sinai—unassailable, unchangeable. But then, amazingly, incredibly, Jesus dared to improve it.

"You have heard that it was said, 'Do not murder.' . . . *But I tell you* that anyone who is angry with his brother will be subject to judgment" (5:21-22, emphasis added).

"You have heard that it was said, 'Do not commit adultery.' . . . *But I tell you* that anyone who looks at a woman lustfully has already committed adultery with her in his heart" (5:27-28, emphasis added).

"You have heard that it was said, 'Do not break your oath.' . . . *But I tell you,* Do not swear at all" (5:33-34, emphasis added).

"You have heard that it was said, 'Eye for eye, and tooth for tooth.' . . . *But I tell you,* Do not resist an evil person" (5:38-39, emphasis added).

"You have heard that it was said, 'Love your neighbor and

hate your enemy.' *But I tell you:* Love your enemies and pray for those who persecute you" (5:43-44, emphasis added).

Of all the religious authorities of Jesus' day, even those who claimed to be Messiah (there were others), none of them dared to take the sacred Law of Moses and add to, improve on or redefine it. Jesus did so, and at the end of His teaching, people were "amazed" (7:28). *What authority?* they thought. Says *who*? And Jesus Himself anticipated the objections of blasphemy: "Do not think that I have come to abolish the Law or the Prophets; I have not come to abolish them but to fulfill them" (5:17).

Still. "Fulfill"? Who would dare say that? Jesus was saying that the Law of Moses is true and valid, but that He would take His listeners to a new level.

And "I have come"? Come from where? Jesus' opponents knew exactly where he came from: right over there, around the shore and up that cliff—Nazareth. But probably almost everybody knew that Jesus wasn't referring to His hometown.

Whom should I believe? is not a merely academic question. We will, consciously or unconsciously, pick and choose between which television network news we deem to be the most reliable and which newspapers, columnists and other opinion makers hold the greatest sway in our minds. But on what basis?

If we're honest about it, we'll admit that we often believe just what we want to believe. So some people prefer journalism that is flat and bland (just the facts), while others look for the energy that comes from point-of-view reporting. And others want point-of-view reporting with explosive passion. If it feels right, it must be true. Or if it stirs up my anger, it must be true because there must be a good reason I'm so agitated about the way things are. And so we read the biased report as unbiased if it strengthens a position we already hold, and we deem a simple reporting of facts as terribly biased if the facts are ones we don't want to look at.

Here is the dilemma: If it is true that as human beings our deepest drive is to believe—to *want* to believe—then that drive can carry us into our own preconceived and prejudged beliefs, and we get nowhere. Instead of being carried by the drive to believe into new beliefs, new understandings of life, new insights, new questions we didn't even know were questions, we will stay contained in a small world we constructed perhaps years ago and don't intend to wander from. But that is like Christopher Columbus loading the Niña, the Pinta and the Santa Maria and sailing in circles off the coast of Portugal, instead of setting off for the high seas.

And that is one more reason why the question of what to believe always comes back to a "who" question. The men who set sail with Columbus believed he had enough credibility to get into the ships with him. They may have wondered if they would fall off the edge of the earth, but they had enough faith to say, "This man, this sailor, is worth trusting. Let's go with him in search of a faster route to Asia."

They didn't realize that he was taking them to a whole New World.

Living a discerning life becomes an intensely practical issue when we realize that every day we make choices based on our perception of who and what we can believe. Trust Doctor A or Doctor B? Seek an attorney or go it on your own? Take the marital advice of this expert or that expert? Go to church or don't go to church? Believe the Bible or assume its words lost relevance a long time ago?

And when you decide whom you can believe, can you
know for certain?

Knowing for Certain

There is a parody religion started in 2005 that says that there exists a unique being in the universe called the Flying Spaghetti Monster who created the world. In this religion, pirates—so badly misunderstood in the past—are "absolute divine beings," and the Ten Commandments become the eight "I'd Really Rather You Didn'ts." *The Gospel of the Flying Spaghetti Monster* was published in 2006. It includes an artistic adaptation of Michelangelo's *The Creation of Adam* in which the figure of God is replaced by a being consisting entirely of meatballs and spaghetti.[1]

This satire sprung from the imagination of a physics graduate student named Bobby Henderson to protest against those who wanted to have Intelligent Design, the theory that a "designer" created the universe, taught in public classrooms. (He calls his Flying Spaghetti Monster theory of the universe's origins Pastafarianism, a combination of the words "pasta" and "Rastafarian.") The point? If someone wants to say that design in the universe is evidence of a designer, why not also assert that there is a divine being consisting of spaghetti and meatballs? There is no more real evidence for that than there is evidence for a Creator God—so says Henderson.

Is it possible to know with certainty that the God and the mission Jesus spoke about is true, and that you can have faith in it all? How does one know it isn't just fantasy? The difference between faith based on fancy and faith based on fact is a matter of evidence. Anyone may choose to believe that a wild dream they had one night was really a ride in an alien spacecraft into which they were abducted, but where is the evidence for it?

As far as I can tell, I do not have arbitrary reasons for believing that Jesus is Lord eternally and that His mission really was authenticated by His teachings, miracles and rising from the dead. I know I could view it as socially beneficial to just go along with this widely held faith conviction. But I also know that there is a certain allure to being an agnostic. The agnostic says, "I won't say that there is a God, and I won't say there isn't. I just don't know." Agnosticism offers the apparently safe route between not insulting a God-who-might-be and not having to regard the limitations on freedom that a faith commitment involves. What is really being said is, "If You're out there God, I have no problem with that, but since You've not made Yourself more obvious, I will live with You as a hypothetical." (Of course, that *really* means living as if God doesn't exist.) Agnosticism has the appearance of open-mindedness and politeness—not being against God, but not being for God either. But you have to stop and ask yourself, *If there really is a Creator God who wonderfully shaped this incredible universe and humanity at its apex and who lovingly has helped humanity out of its self-imposed dilemmas, how would that God respond to the polite doubts of agnosticism?*

It was in the spring of 1869 that English philosopher Thomas Huxley invented the term "agnostic" to make the point that there is an intermediate position between atheism and faith. He wanted to take the position that we cannot know the divine, but we shouldn't exclude the possibility of a divinity. Huxley's brand of agnosticism has the practical effect of saying, "If You're out there God, I'll assume You'll keep to Your corner of the universe, and that leaves me to my own world without having to bother with You."

On the other hand, some take the agnosticism position not because they are intentionally stiff-arming God, but because they are just living in the grayness of uncertainty. "I want to believe" is still there, but it's muted and easy to ignore.

What I cannot ignore is the evidence that comes from the life of Jesus and has had a world-transforming effect in the centuries since He lived on Earth. The core of the evidence for Christian faith comes from the life of Jesus Himself, and His life is described in the documents known as the Gospels.

The person who provided the longest account of the life and times of Jesus was a man named Luke, a physician and traveling companion of Paul the apostle (a special representative of Jesus). Luke was a Gentile, and someone who had access to many eyewitnesses of the life and activities of Jesus. We get a keen insight into the motives and methods of the chroniclers of Jesus when we read the opening words of Luke's Gospel:

Many have undertaken to draw up an account of the things that have been fulfilled among us, just as they were handed down to us by those who from the first were eyewitnesses and servants of the word. Therefore, since I myself have carefully investigated everything from the beginning, it seemed good also to me to write an orderly account for you, most

excellent Theophilus, so that you may *know the certainty* of the things you have been taught (vv. 1-4,
emphasis added).

Knowing with certainty is the issue. This is what Luke
wanted for his friend Theophilus, and it is what we want.
Who doesn't want to live his or her life with a sense of certainty? We want to be as certain as we can be that the person
we choose to marry is the right one. We want certainty about
our financial security in our old age. We want to be certain
that our friends will not betray us. But the reality is that all
of these things may disappoint us, and people who thought
we were sure and dependable may end up disappointed in
us. And so we have the unfortunate aphorism "Nothing is
certain in life." But uncertainty in life shouldn't compel us
to give up and turn cynical. If we give up on being certain
about anything in life, we choose to live the life of a jellyfish
being pushed back and forth by the waves.

The very notion of God is that there is someone somewhere who does not change, is essentially and unalterably
good, who has intent and purpose and intelligence far beyond what we will ever be capable of. Looking for certainty
in God is not wishful thinking; there are many things in
God's creation that are so amazingly predictable that they
become clues that there is a truly immutable Creator. We
are able to aim a rocket into the heavens that will intersect
the planet Mars two years later and land a roving robot
within a mile of a target planned years earlier. There is
amazing human ingenuity behind that, but more amazing
still are the laws of physics governing things like gravity
and motion and the cosmic clockwork that allow us to aim

at an empty spot in space and two years later hit Mars.

Human beings are not so predictable. The outcome of a war can turn out differently than the ideals going into it. Boyfriends and girlfriends disappoint and betray. Believers in Jesus take the purity of who He is and what He taught and (in one of the greatest tragedies in human history) twist it into forms of Christianity that bear little resemblance to God's character. But for all of that, the way of the cynic, who gives up on the potential for virtue in the human race or the goodness of God, is a spiritual death sentence.

There are shockingly disappointing things that happen in life, for sure. And then there is a man like Wesley Autrey, a 50-year-old Harlem construction worker who saw a young man having convulsions fall onto the New York subway tracks, and a train bearing down on his position. In an instant, Autrey jumped on top of the man, pinning him into the two-foot gap between the tracks as the train passed above them both with just inches to spare. Autrey's comment afterward: "I did what anybody would do."[2] No, that's not exactly true; not *anybody* would have done that. But the fact that *somebody* would do it is the headline story, which, like a lantern held up at night, spoils the darkness of the world for at least a little while.

This is what the persecuting Roman emperors did not understand. The more they threw Christians to the lions or burned them at the stake or covered their bodies with tar and made them human torches for the night games, the more faith in Jesus spread like its own kind of fire. Nero will make you a cynic, but the martyrs will make you a believer.

So this physician named Luke, who lived among the first and second generation of Christians, wrote to a man named

Chapter 5

Theophilus a lengthy and compelling account of the life of
Jesus and said that his motive was "so that you may know
the certainty of the things you have been taught." We don't
know who Theophilus was, but his name means "lover of
God," and Luke undoubtedly had a wider audience than this
one man in mind. The Gospel was written to anyone who is
seeking God because he or she has sensed the allure of God.
Theolphilus knew some things about Jesus, but the written
account filled in the gaps.

Luke says, "Many have undertaken to draw up an
account of the things that have been fulfilled among us, just
as they were *handed down* to us by those who from the first
were *eyewitnesses* and servants of the word" (emphasis added). This tells us several things. First, there were many people talking about the amazing life and times of Jesus in the
days that followed His death and resurrection. It should not
surprise us that it was believers in Jesus who left accounts of
His life, not investigative journalists and objective historians. There were no journalists at the time, and historians
wrote about what interested them—usually the splashy,
bloody political events, not things like the small mustard
seed of Jesus' ministry, which they would have considered
peasant rumor.

There were close-in observers who passed along bits and
pieces of the story, most of it in oral form because that was
considered the normal and reliable way of passing on a story.
But Luke distinguishes himself. He says he has written the
things that were "handed down" to him by the "eyewitnesses" of the events. "Handed down" is a technical term for the
careful transmission of an authoritative, defining story.[3] In
other words, the story of Jesus, as reported by Luke and the

other Gospel writers is not a collection of rumors and hear-say. The details were "handed down," so they appear in the four Gospels—Matthew, Mark, Luke and John—many of the details overlapping, but each Gospel writer choosing the parts of the story he wanted to tell. Luke had access to "eye-witnesses," the immediate followers of Jesus, who could say exactly what happened and when and why.

Some scholars have suggested that the so-called Gnostic gospels ought to be taken as seriously as the Gospels in the canon of Scripture (Matthew, Mark, Luke and John). But the Gnostic gospels have a very different character and were written much later than the canonical Gospels. They bring in a bevy of new stories and teachings, but are they inven-tions or facts? Some scholars today say this: The Gnostic gospels are cultural and religious reflections of the commu-nities that told those stories and wrote them down—and the same thing must be said of the canonical Gospels. They say that whether a gospel was written 50 years after the events (like the New Testament) or 300 years after the events (like the Gnostic gospels), they are all just collections of religious ideals that are not based in facts, but rather a thick soup of fabricated Jesus stories and Jesus teachings.

Some critics of the Bible reason that we cannot take the Gospel accounts seriously because they were written by people who were believers in Jesus and His divine authori-ty and power. They were proponents of a position. They had an agenda.

This is true. But Luke calls his sources both "eyewitness-es" and "servants of the word." It is pure circular reasoning to say that because the eyewitnesses became believers, their accounts cannot be taken seriously. If I was out golfing all by myself late in the day and got a hole in one and told my news to some random people at the clubhouse, they may have a hard time believing my account because my testimony would appear self-aggrandizing. And if I said I got two holes in one, they would really be skeptical, not because it's an impossibility but because it is highly unlikely that it would happen.

That is why Luke talks about "eyewitnesses." The Jesus story is not like someone claiming he got a couple of holes in one on one round of golf. There were many people who saw what Jesus did and heard what Jesus said.

The Gospel writers say this about the extraordinary life of Jesus: A man showed up who could work miracles and whose teaching arrested people's attention and who called Himself Son of God and Son of Man. We know this is unlikely. It is unique. But it is not impossible, and the coming of a Savior turns out to be consistent with the instinctual longings of many in the human race.

Luke says he "carefully investigated" the whole story so that he could provide "an orderly account." The early believers in Jesus knew that their message would seem implausible to people. Jesus was not the kind of Messiah anybody was expecting. The idea of miraculous healings fit into the category of magicians' tricks. And this thing about the empty tomb and coming back to life was over the top.

Was the Jesus story a fabrication? Fancy? Fact? We might stop and consider this: If you and some co-conspirators wanted to fabricate a spiritual story and even a new religion, is this the kind of thing you'd come up with? Would you invent a belief system that insulted people's sensitivities by calling them sinners, by propping up a Messiah who had no wealth, no army, no fame, who did not with bared teeth bat-

tle the evil empire? Would you pass on teachings that sometimes were straightforward and clear (for example, "You cannot serve both God and Money" [Matt. 6:24]) and other
times were enigmatic (for example, "Whoever finds his life
will lose it" [Matt. 10:39])?

And would you stay committed to that story and that
faith months and years later when the Founder was nowhere
to be seen (now resurrected and ascended), when the only
organization left behind was a random group of former fish-
ermen, tax collectors, prostitutes and political terrorists—
not really an organization at all, but an association of people
on the run? Would you stay committed to a fiction after the
leader was crucified and His two most influential followers
(Peter and Paul) were themselves imprisoned and executed
in the years that followed?

If you really wanted to invent a religion, wouldn't it be
one that was easy to follow and offered wealth and health
and a good feeling all the time (which, sadly, is the way
Christian faith is sometimes refashioned, giving people a
temporary rush of hope but always leading to a crash, like a
person getting on the heroin roller coaster). All invented religion is toxic, and invented gods are at best phantoms we
dreamed up.

Luke wanted to "carefully investigate" and provide "an
orderly account" precisely because he knew the implausi-
bility of the Jesus narrative and the possibility that with the
passing decades, the fresh information about what really
happened would get corrupted by abridgment and aug-
mentation.

That did eventually happen. In recent years, many people have taken an interest in the so-called Gnostic gospels

such as the Gospel of Thomas and the Gospel of Mary and even a so-called Gospel of Judas. Even a recently discovered ossuary (stone coffin) bearing an inscription in Aramaic (*Ya'akov bar Yosef akhui di Yeshua*, "James, son of Joseph, brother of Jesus") attracted a lot of attention, even though it was shown later to be a modern forgery and hoax. The Jesus story is so important and so captivating, it shouldn't surprise us that any promise of any new hint of evidence about the life of Jesus would be pounced on. Really, this just shows how compelling the presence of Jesus in history really is.

This is why we have ended up in the past 200 years or so with various searches for "the historical Jesus." Like archaeologists digging through layers of dirt to get back to at least a few foundation stones of long-buried structures, historians keep looking for the real Jesus. But that "real" is based on the terms presumed by the diggers. Many have decided before they start digging that the reality of what happened in the early first century in Galilee and Judea may have involved a radical unofficial rabbi and apocalyptic prophet— but not the Son of God come to this world to rescue people from the ravages of sin and evil, ushering in a whole new age of divine power and glory. They have discounted any piece of evidence that points to God-involvement before they lift the first shovel-full of dirt.

So how far have we traveled from the possibility of "certainty" in any sense of the word?

Here are some indisputable facts:

- Followers of Jesus who lived in His era and in all the centuries since have been so certain that Jesus Christ is God's Son, the Savior, Lord of all and risen from the dead, that they have staked their lives on it. Jesus' earliest followers were willing to be put to death for their faith, and it just doesn't make sense that they would do that for a story that they themselves knew was fabricated.

- As Frank Morison concluded in his classic book *Who Moved the Stone?*, there is no more plausible explanation for the empty tomb of Jesus but that He really did rise from the dead.[4] His enemies would have no motive for removing the body, and if they had, they could have produced it to quell the quickly spreading word of a resurrection. He could not have fainted away on the cross and then revived in the tomb, rolling back the stone covering it. Jesus' disciples, whose whole reason for following Jesus was a search for the truth, would not have stolen the body and then made up a story about a resurrection.

- Across the centuries, whole civilizations and the institutions of civilization have been shaped by the message and values of Jesus: truth, justice, mercy, the value and dignity of the individual. Hospitals and schools have been invented out of a Christian milieu. Some of the most dramatic humanitarian responses to human need in the face of disaster have come through Christian communities, like the vast network of churches that were the best first-responders and long-term healers in the aftermath of Hurricane Katrina.

· Countless millions of people have lived their lives
at a higher moral and spiritual plane because of
their faith in Christ, notwithstanding the reality
that, all too often, disreputable people (including
religious leaders) misbehave while polishing themselves with the Name of Jesus. God should not be
blamed for people who misuse His Name. In the
main, people live on a higher plane when they come
under the truth and forgiving grace of Christ.

The list could go on. Some people will consider this evidence, and it will connect with their innate desire to believe.
Others have decided long ago that anything or anyone that
claims certainty is offering a dud deal. They have either settled into indifference because it's the easy way, or they have
made a commitment to uncertainty in principle, via the philosophy of deconstruction or rooted in the world of physics
(as in Heisenberg's uncertainty principle).

Uncertainty is not new—the lauding of uncertainty as a
life-position is. But authentic and honest faith combines
conviction with humility. Faith looks at the evidence and
says, as did the man who brought his sick boy to Jesus, "I do
believe; help me overcome my unbelief!" (Mark 9:24).

The Message of Jesus

In the chapters ahead we will continue to look at the experience of belief, but more important, we will look at some specific belief systems and compare them with the message of
Jesus. But what was that message? What is it that is at the

core of Christianity—or ought to be, if Christianity is based on the teachings of Jesus?

When Jesus talked and His followers wrote about the substance of belief, they offered a complete structure for life that directly connected beliefs about God with beliefs about the purpose of our lives and the practical decisions we face everyday. Here are the contours of Jesus-faith, to be described in greater detail in later chapters:

1. *The universe as we know it is the creation of a unique divine being we know as God.* This self-existent, self-governing, self-sustaining Being has existed from all eternity. He is all-powerful, all-knowing and present everywhere. He created the world and its creatures, including human beings, as an act of His will. God delighted to bring the universe into existence, and the whole universe reflects God's grandeur and glory.

2. Although the universe was created good ("It is good" is repeated again and again in the Creation account in the book of Genesis), *the free humans God created had the option to live in harmony with God or to rebel against Him.* Tragically, this has been the experience of the human race from the start: Sometimes living harmoniously with God, sometimes giving in to greed, jealousy, aggression, avarice and a host of other vices, human beings have shown this paradoxical two-sided nature. They can reflect the glory of God in acts of love and selflessness and creative ingenuity,

but motives are almost always mixed—human beings are always only a step away from broken relationships, self-destructive compulsions and hopelessness.

3. God could not look at the brokenness of human society with indifference because He cares about what He created. *God loved the world so much that He sent someone who could be the Rescuer and Savior the human race needs.* God sent "His only begotten Son" (John 3:16), whom we know as Jesus from Nazareth, Jesus the Christ. In a great mission, Jesus taught and showed how God's benevolent reigning power was coming into the world in a bold new way. This good news about "the kingdom of God" was the promise that God would offer restoration to broken human beings. The teachings of Jesus (which people recognized as having an extraordinary ring of truth to them) and the miracles He performed were demonstrations of this new era of God's kingdom.

4. Jesus' short-lived public life was dramatic and life-transforming for many, but it ended with His execution on trumped-up charges of sedition. But the death of Jesus was not just another martyrdom. A "work" was accomplished in His sacrifice. As pre-figured in the sacrificial system we read about in the Old Testament, *Jesus' death was a once-for-all sacrifice and substitution on behalf of human beings who needed to be reconciled to God.*

5. *The followers of Jesus witnessed and proclaimed that they found His tomb empty on the third day after His execution.* There were sightings of a resurrected Jesus. None of Jesus' opponents quelled the rumors, though all they would have had to do is produce the body of Jesus. It is not plausible that the resurrection of Jesus was a ruse perpetrated by His followers—they would not have died martyrs' deaths in the years that followed for a lie they had fabricated.

6. Followers of Jesus look back to His promises of a place in the home of God in the future, the state that we enter on the other side of death. Though the details of that life are incomprehensible to us now, it is not at all implausible that *the Creator who gave us life in the first place will preserve it beyond our time in these bodies.*

7. *Generations of followers of Jesus, who believe they live by the guidance and gifting of the Holy Spirit of God, have believed that their lives are better for the freedom that comes from the forgiveness of sins, and they are committed to an ongoing mission to keep the news about Jesus Christ spreading to people without God and without hope.* This message rang so true in the early decades after Jesus that the Jesus-faith spread like wildfire. Amazingly, it became the majority faith in the Roman Empire within the first two centuries, and then went on to spread all over the world, becoming the most widely held belief system today.

8. Unfortunately, many people across the centuries have taken the name "Christian" with no real living connection with Christ. When "Christian" becomes a merely cultural or nationalistic description, when it is without content or real faith, then others see "Christianity" as a mixed blessing—sometimes quite removed from the message of Jesus. *Many "Christians" have promoted a faith that has lost the essential connection with the message of Jesus.*

9. *The Bible, including the Hebrew Old Testament, and the Christian New Testament, are believed to be God's revelation for faith and life.* The Bible is the Word of God—not equivalent to God Himself, but flowing directly from the mind and heart of God, a divine word, spoken through human prophets and apostles. The Bible gives definition to life (although it must be read and interpreted carefully), and speaks consistently of a future time when God will remake the Creation.

10. *Christian faith looks forward to that dividing line in history when Christ will return to initiate a process of recreating heaven and Earth.* In the meantime the world remains a place of blessing and curse, of peace and bitter conflict. Christian faith always hopes for the best—that more and more people will receive the life-changing blessings of the Christ life—while not assuming anything. Evil and wickedness will continue until God interrupts human history. The age in which we live really is "the best of times and the worst of times."

The Christian says not just "I want to believe," but also "I believe *this*." But what happens when doubt casts its long shadow over faith?

Notes

1. Bobby Henderson, *The Gospel of the Flying Spaghetti Monster* (New York: Villard, 2006).

2. Wesley Autrey, interview by Randi Kaye, *CNN News*, January 4, 2007. Transcripts available online at http://transcripts.cnn.com/TRANSCRIPTS/0701/04/cnr.05.html (accessed June 2007).

3. See note on "authoritative" in the *NIV Study Bible* (Grand Rapids, MI: Zondervan, 2002), p. 1533.

4. Frank Morison, *Who Moved the Stone?* (London: Faber & Faber, 1962).

CHAPTER 6

Doubt

Doubt is not the opposite of belief—it is simply the horizon between what we know with certainty today and what we hope becomes clearer in the future. I am glad when I have the opportunity to speak with people who have doubts about their faith, because that is what Jesus spent a lot of His time doing.

Christopher Hitchens doubts that God exists. Actually, that's a huge understatement. Hitchens, a noted journalist and literary critic, positively *dis*believes in the existence of God. And he *wants* to disbelieve. On a television talk show, Hitchens told NBC journalist Tim Russert that he doesn't believe in God because he thinks there is no evidence for it, but then went on to say:

> And I don't want it to be the case, that there is a divine superintending celestial dictatorship from which I could never escape and that abolishes my private life . . . that would supervise me, keep me under surveillance in every moment of my living existence. And then, when I died, it would be like living in a heavenly North Korea where one's only duty was to continue to abase oneself and to thank forever the dear leader for everything that we are and have.[1]

Hitchens does not believe and says straight out that he doesn't *want* to believe in God—because he doesn't want to live under a scrutinizing divine dictatorship. But who *would* want to believe in a graceless, loveless, arbitrary God? Hitchens rejects a God or an idea of God that ought to be rejected.

His book *God Is Not Great: How Religion Poisons Everything* got everybody's attention as soon as it was published.[2] Hitchens may not believe in a great God, but he has profited immensely from writing a bestseller about the non-existence of a great God. The book is disbelief written in language that is as big and as blunt as can be. The title says it all. It's not that Hitchens, a thoughtful and articulate person, is incapable of nuance. But this book is so extreme that it's hard to take his main point seriously. Anyone with half a brain would have to admit that *sometimes* religion poisons things— but only if it is a variety that is poisonous. It's hardly fair to take torture in the Inquisition, radical Islamic jihad and fringe practices of ultra-orthodox Jews and say, "This is where religion will get you; this is what it is all about." It isn't logical or reasonable. Atheism is Hitchens's chosen commitment—but while he may point out that many atheists and rationalists are well-behaved, he should not ignore the cruelties of the atheistic regimes of Stalin, Pol Pot and Hitler. A logical interpretation of history dictates that you cannot judge Christianity (or other religions) based on their worstcase manifestations—and you cannot take some examples of good-natured, well-meaning atheists as an endorsement of the complete rejection of God.

Some people—not many—are absolute in their disbelief (by Hitchens's own estimation, probably only 2 percent of people in the U.S. hold to his brand of complete atheism).

The vast majority of people are believers in some sense, and carry on in life with a conviction of the presence and the goodness of God. But what do we say about the experience of doubt? What is it? Why does it happen? What can a person do with nagging doubt? Is doubt a sin against God?

As I mentioned, I am glad when I have the opportunity to speak with people who have doubts about their faith. Now, don't get me wrong—I'm not glad about the pain that they experience in one of the most intimate issues of life. And that pain can be intense—like that felt by a husband or wife who overhears whispering hints that his or her spouse has been cheating. Or like the pain that follows the death of a loved one. Conversations with people who doubt are often halting, quiet, scattered. I have never met someone of faith who *wanted* to have doubts about their faith, because it really isn't about doubting faith—it's about doubting God. People don't want to doubt God; they just have questions that come up in life that hang in the air like half-inflated helium balloons. Sometimes they feel like they can't look past them—they want some answers.

For many, doubt is like driving into a fog. You didn't see it coming, but now you're in it. You don't know how to get out of it, you don't know what way to turn, and you don't even remember exactly where you were when you got into it. You didn't ask for the fog—it's just how things are.

The reason I say I'm glad for those conversations is that it is better for someone experiencing doubt to talk to someone than to let doubt fester. Like grief, doubt itself does not injure; it is often the result of injury. And we need to know this: Our doubts do not injure God, because nothing can injure God. It is possible to insult God—because any of us are capable of disrespect—but apparently doubt in the form of sincere questioning is not an insult to God. The Bible never says that the moment we waver, God is ready to cut us off. The Bible is one long story of human beings living on the horizon between faith and doubt, interacting with their Creator—all the time showing their inclination: "I *want* to believe." Doubt is not a contradiction of faith. It is its precursor.

But ultimately the question we need to answer is, *How are we going to deal with doubt?* The answer is different for the habitual doubt of the utter skeptic and the passing doubt of the believer who has been tossed into uncertainty because of a life crisis. But in either case, the only effective response to doubt is to get rooted in real faith.

There is a passionate plea in the middle of the book of Colossians in the New Testament, in which the apostle Paul says:

> Just as you received Christ Jesus as Lord, continue to live [literally, "walk"] in him, rooted and built up in him, strengthened in the faith as you were taught, and overflowing with thankfulness. See to it that no one takes you captive through hollow and deceptive philosophy, which depends on human tradition and the basic principles of this world rather than on Christ. For in Christ all the fullness of the Deity lives in bodily form, and you have been given fullness in Christ, who is the head over every power and authority (2:6-10).

There is nothing better that can happen to a person in life than to come to the place of saying "I believe." It is like someone has turned the lights on, or better yet, the day has dawned and the confusion and oppression of the darkness of life has been pushed back.

We want to believe because without faith all we're left with is a gigantic question mark about the meaning and purpose of life, no real hope for the future, and no assurance that we are loved by anyone beyond passing human affection. Without faith we are cut off from our Creator, and consequently, we are cut off from what He has created. All of life becomes disjointed. It is like sitting on a stool where two of the three legs have become loose and the whole thing could collapse at any moment.

If we want to believe, then we need to realize that faith doesn't happen in a moment; it is a lifelong walk. Those who receive Jesus as Lord need to begin and continue a walk with Him. When you put these two ideas together—receiving and walking—you get a total picture of faith. It is not just walking, as if it were up to us to go on a great quest in order to find God who is hidden up high in the mountains somewhere; but neither is it only receiving, which would be like repeating vows in a wedding ceremony but not following through with marital commitment.

Many believers are fond of speaking in terms of "receiving" Christ, and that is biblical, as we see in the passage from Colossians. But it is only one way of describing the reality of faith. And it is important that we realize just how serious this receiving is. It is not merely saying the right words or praying the right prayer as if they were some kind of incantation. While it is true that the front end of receiving the Lord Jesus is a simple admission of need—a plea for mercy, an opening of heart and hands—we should realize that receiving a lord means to give up one's own lordship of life. (And we would do well to eliminate from our vocabulary the phrase "making Christ Lord." We don't *make* Him anything. If Christ is Lord, He is Lord whether we acknowledge it or not.) Then the walk begins. Just one step after another. Not worrying about whether or not we'll make it to the top of the mountain of life, because God will inevitably have to carry us some of the way and will bring us to the summit in the end.

How do you deal with doubt? You tell yourself that you're not inventing faith, that you don't have to have all of life's questions answered today, that you don't need to figure out exactly where you will be five years from now. God knows. You just have to take the next step.

Now, to switch metaphors, there is tremendous assurance that if you are on the walk of faith with Christ as Lord, you're doing the right thing because you have been "rooted and built up" and "strengthened." Every time you have the sense of being uprooted by some tornado that has come through your life—a sudden and unexpected loss, a betrayal, a time of doubt—you can recall that you are not like a willow tree, with shallow roots, susceptible to every passing storm. You—by God's work—are like an elm or oak with a massive root system that goes deep and holds fast. The healthy life of faith is both about the foliage and fruit at the top, and the strength and health in the roots.

When something happens that tears us down, we have the assurance that we have been "rooted and built up" and "strengthened" in Christ. We didn't build the superstructure of faith. It is God's truth, and we live in the shelter of it.

All of this leads to thanksgiving, and that too keeps us walking in the right direction. When we have a strong sense of gratitude for what God has meant and what God has done in the tough times and in the easy times, the act of thanksgiving keeps us looking up. Many of the psalms say, "I lift up my eyes" (Pss. 121:1; 123:1) because that is when we can see God ahead of us. Carrying a chip on your shoulder because you think God hasn't done enough lately undercuts any effort to get closer to God or be strengthened by Him.

That brings us to a second point mentioned in this passage from Colossians: the challenge of "hollow philosophies" that can have a captivating allure but that are essentially deceptions. Dealing with doubt is sometimes a matter of dismay and discouragement because of life's difficulties, but sometimes doubt is the wreckage resulting from deception.

The phenomenally bestselling novel *The Da Vinci Code* by Dan Brown presented a very new and very old non-gospel (by that I mean that there is very little good news in Brown's story). The fiction is clearly in the foreground, as is the case with all novels, but the historical background about who Jesus really was and is takes the twisted shape of conspiracy and cover-up. The Lord of heaven and Earth is demoted to the level of a good man, a husband and father, who produced a progeny but no legacy. One of the strangest things about Dan Brown's story is that it makes Jesus a mere mortal and then doesn't even bother to make Him a notable mortal. In the film version, the edge is taken off—maybe it's okay to pray to this Jesus (it can't really do any harm), but that's up to you. "The only thing that matters is what you believe," says one of the film's characters.

But here is what really riveted my attention when I read the novel. The last paragraphs of *The Da Vinci Code* have the main character, Robert Langdon, standing at the place where the bones of Mary Magdalene (in the story) may be found. Brown writes:

> Like the murmurs of spirits in the darkness, for-
> gotten words echoed. The quest of the Holy Grail
> is the quest to kneel before the bones of Mary
> Magdalene. . . . With a sudden upwelling of rever-
> ence, Robert Langdon fell to his knees. For a mo-
> ment, he thought he heard a woman's voice . . .
> the wisdom of the ages . . . whispering up from the
> chasms of the earth.[3]

The implication of these climactic lines is that something good for our lives can come from "murmurs of spirits
in the darkness" and "whispering up from the chasms of the
earth." I wonder how many people really want to believe
that conclusion.

If we're living in an age of faith, we are also living in an age
of doubt. Sometimes doubt arises because of personal crisis
(that's just one kind of situation), but some of the time doubt
takes hold because the philosophies of human invention and
spiritual deception are setting the agenda of the day. And then
it all gets mixed up with who has the right to say what. And
people think that Christians are just too uptight and not
open-minded enough and want to be too controlling.

Here, briefly, is the story of the search for faith since the
coming of Jesus. The first-century world into which Jesus
came offered a potpourri of religions and philosophies.
Rather like today, the Greco-Roman world had a religion on
every corner and a philosopher's school on every street. And
in that dynamic mix, the message of who Jesus is and what

He accomplished and what He offers spread like nothing before. A whole civilization developed out of that faith; but along the way, the Church, at different times, misrepresented Jesus and was an all-too-human institution.

That brings us to the modern era, when in the 1700s and 1800s people turned to reason as a better alternative than religion. Science became the way to true knowledge—the only source of knowledge, really. But as the war-torn decades of the twentieth century unfolded, a lot of people found that "modernism" cold and without meaning. You can't get a purpose for life out of a test tube. And with this "postmodern" mindset, people have said, "Maybe we should go looking for God again; maybe supernatural things have happened; maybe Jesus is important. Let's go looking."

The Gnostic movement of the third and fourth centuries tried to reinterpret Jesus, but it became the opportunity for people to be curious and to look back to the first century and look at the first beliefs of the early Christians.

Colossians 2:9-12 says:

> For in Christ all the fullness of the Deity lives in bodily form, and you have been given fullness in Christ, who is the head over every power and authority. In him you were also circumcised, in the putting off of the sinful nature, not with a circumcision done by the hands of men but with the circumcision done by Christ, having been buried with him in baptism and raised with him through your faith in the power of God, who raised him from the dead.

What is the fullness of deity in Jesus? And how can it be? Is it a mystery? Absolutely. Is it beyond our comprehension?

Yes. But this is exactly what you'd expect a good God to do.

Yet the best news of all is this: Human beings have been offered "fullness" in Christ. Not the fullness of deity. God remains God and we remain human. Human is not divine any more than a pot is the same as the potter or the painting is the same as the painter. But the Christian gospel—the really good news of the day—says this: In Christ you can have the fullness of everything you really need.

It all begins with God forgiving you for your faults and shortcomings and sins. This is not an easy forgiveness. For our sakes, the innocent Son of God went through humiliation and suffering and a death He should not have been subject to. And so He says to us, *To be forgiven, you have to go through a kind of death yourself.* Baptism is a picture of this burial of the old self so that a new self can emerge. And if you die to yourself—in the sense of giving up your personal prerogatives, your arbitrary and imaginative ideas of who God is—then you will surely be raised by the power of God to live a new life.

Notes

1. Christopher Hitchens, from an interview with Tim Russert, CNBC, June 30, 2007.
2. Christopher Hitchens, *God Is Not Great: How Religion Poisons Everything* (New York: Twelve, Hachette Book Group, 2007).
3. Dan Brown, *The Da Vinci Code* (New York: Doubleday, 2003), p. 454.

CHAPTER 7

If You Meet the Buddha on the Road

Just a few years ago, the powerhouse of the National Basketball Association was the Chicago Bulls. Michael Jordan reigned over the court, led by an amazing coach, Phil Jackson, who led them on to three championships in a row. Along the way, the public learned that behind Coach Jackson's winning ways was a philosophy of life called Zen Buddhism, which he wrote about in *Sacred Hoops: Spiritual Lessons of a Hardwood Warrior.*

> In basketball—as in life—true joy comes from being fully present in each and every moment. . . . The day I took over the Bulls, I vowed to create an environment based on the principles of selflessness and compassion I'd learned as a Christian in my parents' home; sitting on a cushion practicing Zen; and studying the teachings of the Lakota Sioux. I knew that the only way to win consistently was to give everybody—from the stars to the number 12 player on the bench—a vital role on the team. . . . More than anything, I wanted to build a team that would blend individual talent with a heightened group consciousness.[1]

Who could argue with a winner? If you can blend Christian compassion with Buddhist higher consciousness, maybe that shows that the world's religions are not really at war with each other but can be blended into a winning approach to life.

The issue of this chapter and the four that follow is, *What are we to make of the different religions?* Why are there so many different religions and should we assume that one is right and all the others are wrong? What if you're a Christian and you read something by Coach Jackson that sounds true? Are there points of intersection between Christian faith and Buddhism or Islam or Hinduism?

Of course, the real question that so many people want an answer to today is, *Is there really only one way to God and one way to heaven, or are the various religions simply different paths up a mountain that ultimately get to the summit one way or another?*

The very fact that there are one and a half billion Christians, a billion Muslims, a billion Hindus, and other religious adherents numbering in the hundreds of millions in the world today tells us, first of all, that the human race *wants to believe*. Three hundred years ago many European intellectuals who gave up religion for rationalism believed that the human race was finally getting over the infancy of religious-mindedness, and a great many people today believe that the world would be a much better place if somehow we could get rid of religion. But that is not happening. Even with the tremendous advantages of living with ever-deepening scientific knowledge, humanity still wants to find a foundation in the Creator or in immutable spiritual principles. Meteorology allows us to track a killer hurricane bearing down on coastal populations, but we cannot take the power out of the wind.

Cancer research has given us effective treatments for some forms of cancer, but it has not cured it; and even if the cure came one day, we would still live with the reality of our mortality. I drive a car today that has three different air-bag systems, but if a semi-truck broadsides me, I'm definitely going to be launched into the afterlife. Through amniocentesis, doctors can extract tissue from an unborn baby and study the genetic likelihood of diseases and other conditions—even physical characteristics—but what do you do with that knowledge, and what is ethical?

Human beings are spiritual creatures, even if they are unaware of it.

Are all religions the same? No, of course they are not, though there are points of convergence and commonality all around—like the longing for salvation and the search for a God higher than ourselves. Hinduism is not the same as Judaism, and Scientology is not the same as Taoism. As Ravi Zacharias has said in his recent book, *Jesus Among the Gods*:

> All religions are not the same. All religions do not point to God. All religions do not say that all religions are the same. At the heart of every religion is an uncompromising commitment to a particular way of defining who God is or is not. . . . Anyone who claims that all religions are the same betrays not only an ignorance of all religions but also a caricatured view of even the best-known ones. Every religion at its core is exclusive.[2]

Some people think they are showing respect by asserting that all religions are basically the same, but that is not respectful to the Christian, the Muslim, the Jew or the Hindu. The Dalai Lama, the leader of Tibetan Buddhism in the world today, has said that trying to combine Christianity and Buddhism (which some have tried to do) "is like putting a yak's head on a sheep's body."[3] He believes that it is valuable to note the areas where the world's religions converge (as, for example, the quest for justice and love), but that ignoring the differences between religions is helpful to no one.

I know that some people reading this will already start to feel skittish. "Here we go again. One religion battling it out with another. One more reminder of why we live in a tension-filled world." But I would like to ask the nervous reader to stop and consider this: In many parts of the world today, people of different religions have perfectly civil discussions with each other about what they believe and why—including the points of divergence. In America, we are so timid about stepping on somebody else's toes that we have largely dropped the skill and spirit of religious discourse. We somehow think it is wrong if a Christian and a Hindu get into a spirited discussion about what they believe and why their beliefs are different. But it doesn't have to be that way, and such discussions are hugely beneficial for helping people understand exactly what they believe and what people of other religions believe. To run away from discourse about religious convictions because we fear hurting someone else's feelings or because we fear being viewed as bigoted is not respectful of anybody; it is just cowardly. And it makes no sense to pretend that religious streams are not coursing their way through our culture and thoughts all the time. The tenets of many religions are sprinkled throughout our movies, books and even the lives of celebrities who get a lot of attention.

So let's begin, in this chapter, by taking the case of Buddhism. I am a Christian, not a Buddhist, but I sincerely want to know about this philosophy that hundreds of millions of people in the world hold to today—and I want to know accurately what they believe.

More than 500 years before the birth of Jesus, in a remote corner of northeast India, Siddhartha Gautama, the founder of Buddhism, was born into a privileged family of the warrior class. A pampered prince, he married at age 16 or 17 and had a son. At the age of 29, a spiritual longing in Siddhartha led him to consider leaving the comforts of home and taking up the lifestyle of a homeless, traveling seeker. Despite his father's attempt to keep him sheltered from the harsh realities of life, one day Siddhartha came to a park where, over a period of days, he observed in succession a decrepit old man, a diseased man, a dead man and an ascetic—someone who lived the life of self-imposed poverty and who seemed, to Siddhartha, to be decently clad and spiritually happy.

Siddhartha left his home, left his family and began to wander in search of the truth. He began to question some of the religious tenets of Hinduism in which he had grown up: the rituals of the Hindu priests; the caste system that said one had to be a male priest to gain *moksha* (salvation); the many gods that didn't seem to do much good for people. *There must be something better than this,* he thought.

He sought to purge his body of impurities through extreme fasting, believing the physical to be the source of what is bad in life. *Reduce the body, expand the mind,* he thought. He grew so gaunt during one fast, according to one account, he could, by touching his belly, feel his backbone. The hairs on his arms fell off; his skin grew dark. But he did not find spiritual peace. He recalled times, when he was still at home, that he had found more peace through the practice of meditation. So he abandoned his extreme asceticism (losing five disciples who had taken up with him), began to practice a more moderate austerity, which he called "the Middle Way," and turned his focus toward meditation.

What happened next is central to understanding the heart of Buddhism, a movement that would eventually spread throughout India, Korea, Japan and China, making it the most dominant religion in the Asian world today. (In one American state, Hawaii, Buddhism is widely represented.)

Siddhartha went to meditate under a great tree. He entered into an intense personal introspective experience. So deep was this experience that when he came out of it, he claimed to have reached enlightenment. Thus, Siddhartha Gautama became "the Enlightened One," the Buddha (which comes from the Sanskrit word for "enlightenment").

"Buddha" does not mean "God." In fact, one of the surprising things to non-Buddhists is the fact that Buddhism doesn't hold much interest in seeking one true God. Some would say that Buddhism is really a form of atheism, or maybe pantheism. The fact is that the heart and soul of Buddhism is the belief that salvation consists in becoming enlightened. If you yourself find this enlightenment, you too become like Buddha, because there is no one unique Enlightened One. This epiphany of truth comes strictly from within. You don't need a teacher, but you do need the technique of meditation. There is a Buddhist saying: "If you see the Buddha on the road, kill him." In other words, if someone claims to be your teacher, someone who brings enlightenment to you from the outside, reject it. You are your own teacher. The only valid truth is that which comes from within.

Jesus talked about enlightenment, but from a different direction: "I am the light of the world" (John 8:12); "He who believes in me . . ." (John 6:35; 11:25); "If you obey my commands . . ." (John 15:10). In Christianity, hope centers on the belief that help comes to us *from the outside*; we are rescued by God in Christ when we couldn't do it ourselves. Enlightenment is a good thing, but while it is experienced in the inner person, the source of the light comes from without, not from within.

So how did this experience of a young man who believed he found light within himself under a great Bodhi tree grow into a massive world religion?

There is a body of teaching in Buddhism that has been attractive to many people in the world, especially in today's world. Buddha taught that there are Four Noble Truths: (1) Life is fundamentally disappointment and suffering; (2) suffering is a result of one's desires for pleasure, power and continued existence; (3) to stop disappointment and suffering, one must stop desiring; and (4) the way to stop desiring and thus suffering is by following the noble Eightfold Path. And what is the Eightfold Path? Right view, intention, speech, conduct, livelihood, effort, mindfulness and concentration.

When he was about 80 years old, Siddhartha Gautama became gravely ill while on a journey. He told his disciples that they should direct their attention, not toward him, but toward themselves and the truth. He asked them three times if they had any final questions, but each time was met with silence. His last words were, "Decay is inherent in all component things. . . . Work out your salvation with diligence!"[4] His disciples were exhorted to restrain from sorrow, to show passionless composure. For six days after Buddha's death, his followers paid homage with perfumes and garlands and wreaths; and on the seventh day, his body was cremated and divided into eight parts to be enshrined in different political regions of northeast India.

Since the time of Siddhartha Gautama, the spiritual philosophy and discipline of Buddhism has attracted multitudes of people. It has two distinguishing characteristics. First, there is no absolute deity. Either there is no god, or we do not need to be concerned about the issue. Second, karma, reincarnation and nirvana are the driving issues of life. After you die, you come back to life in some other form (that's reincarnation), depending on the quality of the life you presently live (that's karma). And if you achieve enlightenment, that cycle will be finally broken and you will come to nirvana, which is not heaven but simply release from the perpetual cycle of reincarnation, like getting out of a revolving door.

The attraction of Buddhism is that it offers religion without god, philosophy without theology, spiritual activity without spiritual obligation. It emphasizes personal autonomy, enlightenment and contentment. Some believe it can be layered on top of another religion. But remember what the Dalai Lama said about not trying to put a yak's head on a sheep's body. It is ridiculous and insulting to the Jew, the Christian, the Muslim and the Hindu to say that the beliefs of Buddhism are no different from their beliefs or that the belief systems can be joined together with tape and glue.

There are points of overlap between Buddhism and Christianity, like avoiding the dangers of worshiping material wealth and physical well-being. (And there are probably plenty of Buddhists who are more skilled at avoiding materialism than Christians, though Christians likewise believe we must not worship or be trapped by our possessions.) But there are dramatic differences between the two. Buddhism says that you should kill (figuratively) someone you meet on the road who says he is the way (the Buddha). But Jesus said of Himself, "I am the way and the truth and the life" (John 14:6). Siddhartha Buddha said, "Decay is inherent in all component things," whereas Jesus talked about going from this world to a new place where there are many rooms. Not nirvana, not reincarnation, but paradise. And His body, resurrected from the tomb, would not see decay.

Like other mystical religions, Buddhism says that truth and certainty are elusive and, in some ways, exclusive. Jesus, however, talked about certainty. In just one discourse (John 14), Jesus talked about certainty at many different levels, especially certainty about knowledge of God ("Anyone who has seen me has seen the Father. . . . Don't you believe that I am in the Father, and that the Father is in me?" [vv. 9-10]). The Gospels speak of certain knowledge of the Son of God, as in the event of the transfiguration of Jesus when three of His disciples saw Jesus bathed in light and heard a voice from heaven: "This is my Son, whom I love. Listen to him!" (Mark 9:7). And there is the certainty about God's work in the world. Jesus said He came to do the work of God the Father ("It is the Father, living in me, who is doing his work" [John 14:10]), and then, amazingly, He told His followers that they would continue the work, doing "even greater things" (John 14:12). No Christian or group of Christians has done anything "greater" in quality compared to the work of Christ (and, all too often, have worked against His purposes), but "greater" in the sense of broader, as faith in God through Christ has spread all over the world and shaped whole civilizations. In Jesus, there is certain love ("He who loves me will be loved by my Father, and I too will love him and show myself to him" [John 14:21]); certain direction ("Whoever has my commands and obeys them, he is the one who loves me" [John 14:21]); and certain peace ("Peace I leave with you; my peace I give you. . . . Do not let your hearts be troubled and do not be afraid" [John 14:27]).

Is it arrogant to say that you are certain about what you believe? In most times and places, this would be an absurd thought. Of course we want to be certain, and if certainty is at hand, it is a gift too good to ignore. Certainty is only arrogance if its motive is power over others rather than a search for truth. The person who thinks he is a mortal and fallible human being will always hold humility with certainty. Christian faith teaches that as long as we live in this world, we are seeing things as in a dim mirror (see 1 Cor. 13:12). One day we will see Jesus face to face, and that will be the day of perfect knowledge (see 1 John 3:2). In the meantime, our knowledge is incomplete but can be certain.

For a number of years, our family chose to take a vacation in the spectacular Rocky Mountains. Living as we do in the Midwest, we have great bodies of water like Lake Michigan around, which I've lived near my whole life and enjoy immensely. But we have no mountains. We don't live in the dramatic creases or on the crests of those giants. Ours is a flatter life.

As you drive toward a mountain range, you can see the ridge gradually form on the horizon. And then it grows. You know, with certainty, your direction. And even when I chose to get off the boring interstate highway and take smaller roads—the scenic route—and even when I got a little lost, as long as the range was ahead of me, I knew, with certainty, that I was heading in the right direction.

There is nothing arrogant about certainty, as long as the certainty is not coming from ourselves but from the reality of God, who is greater than ourselves.

Notes

1. Phil Jackson and Hugh Delehanty, *Sacred Hoops: Spiritual Lessons of a Hardwood Warrior* (New York: Hyperion, 1995), p. 4.
2. Ravi Zacharias, *Jesus Among the Gods* (Nashville, TN: W Publishing Group, 2000), p. 7.
3. Dalai Lama, *The Good Heart: A Buddhist Perspective on the Teachings of Jesus* (Somerville, MA: Wisdom Publications, 1998), p. 105.
4. Paul Carus, *Buddha, The Gospel* (Chicago, IL: The Open Court Publishing Company, 1894), from the *Internet Sacred Text Archive*. http://www.sacred-texts.com/bud/btg/btg98.htm (accessed June 2007).

CHAPTER 8

The Challenge of Atheism

The starkest religious alternative to Christian faith is atheism. While it may seem strange to even describe atheism as a religious alternative, doing so is accurate because atheism is the dogma that there is no God, a position that usually requires a great deal of talk and debate about God.

At the twenty-fifth annual meeting of the organization called American Atheists, its 44-year-old president strode to the lectern and opened with the words: "Happy Vernal Equinox and good morning. My name is Ellen Johnson and I am the President of American Atheists."[1] A very different picture from the previous president, Madalyn Murray O'Hair (who disappeared in 1995 and was recently confirmed murdered for money), Ellen Johnson is a newer picture of atheism. Slender, blonde, a self-described soccer mom, she nonetheless carries on the message of being freed from the restraints of religion and of wanting tolerance in a free society.

After her introduction she went on to say:

I am a second generation Atheist. When my two sisters and I grew up here in New Jersey, we were not taught to be religious. Everything that my parents said and did reflected an Atheistic approach to life. I don't know if my parents would have called themselves Atheists back then. They just had absolutely no

interest in, or use for, religion. . . . I knew from my earliest recollections that I was an Atheist and my Atheism is something that I hold very dear to my heart. It
has enriched my life and made me a better person
which is probably why I have spent the last twenty
years of my life working to "share the good word or
good news of Atheism," to put a twist on a typical
religious phrase. Although my parents are home and
not here today, I want to say how deeply grateful I
am to them for the Atheist approach to life that they
instilled in me. For those of you who rear your children as Atheists I know that someday they will thank
you for it as well. It is one of the greatest gifts you
can give to them.[2]

American Atheists is not a large organization. Some 2,500
members nationwide are well aware that 95 percent of Americans say they believe in God while only 1 to 2 percent say
they absolutely believe there is no God and no afterlife. Yet
the issue of atheism goes far beyond those who publicly
announce they are atheists.

There are many faces of atheism in the modern world.
A person may be an atheist because of his or her socioeco-
nomic view of life or scientific evaluation of reality or political perspectives or because he or she just simply doesn't
want to have to be answerable to anybody. "I want to live my
life as I wish, and I don't need and don't desire any god to
interfere with that" is the sentiment. The idea of being beholden to God is repugnant or tired and lifeless, so a person
steps off into the open air of disbelief—no matter how
strong are the voices of others or the inner voice that shouts

out, *Worship! Adore! Seek! Trust! Commit!* Atheism shuts down the voice that says, "I want to believe."

One of the great proponents of atheism in the modern world was Karl Marx, the father of socialism. Marx was a materialist, pure and simple. Materialism as a philosophy of life is not what we're referring to when we speak about "being too materialistic." Marx's problem was not that he spent too much time at the mall or adored his BMWs (if they had had malls and BMWs in late nineteenth-century Germany). No, materialism as a worldview says, "I understand what I can touch, see, taste, smell or hear—in other words, the physical or material world. I can measure it, weigh it, sense it. A scientist can observe it and do experiments on it. The sum totality of the physical universe—rocks, trees, oceans, bison, people, moons, stars and stardust—is all there is."

Years ago I remember watching the beginning of a television series called *Cosmos,* done by Carl Sagan, the popular astrophysicist from Cornell University. The first words, intoned by the distinctive voice of Sagan and set against photos of stars, galaxies and fields of flowers, were "The cosmos is all there is or ever was or ever will be." I remember getting a shiver. The statement sounded almost like a creed, like a statement of faith in the materialistic universe and that alone. And, of course, that is precisely what Sagan meant.

Sagan was a proponent of *scientific materialism,* the view that reality can only be discovered through scientific investigation: what can be observed, measured and replicated by experiment. Now, nobody will argue that it is not a good thing when scientists can find treatments for diseases by understanding the chemistry and physiology behind ailments. We all want our skyscrapers to be more earthquake-proof and for the local water utility to know best how to purify the water we drink. Reliable empirical knowledge, achieved by scientific observation, analysis and application, is a good thing. More than that, great science is humanity showing some of its very best talents—God-given as they are.

But some people leap from science to scientific material- ism, or *scientism*. Scientism is the view that science is the *only* means of valid human knowledge. Scientism says, "We are physical creatures in a physical world. Our knowledge comes through our senses, so it is literally non-*sense* to talk about any kind of supernatural knowledge (that is, knowledge be- yond the physical)." That includes, of course, knowledge of God or any kind of spiritual knowledge. The true materialist will tell you that you can speculate about whether there is a God, but there is no way you can ever know, because all knowledge is rooted in sensory experience. "If you could show me God, let me see Him, touch Him, hear Him . . . then I could tell you I believe in Him."

The Christian response is, first, that God is invisible and there are indeed realities that are above the physical, materi- al world. Love, for instance, is something that can't be put in a test tube, but we all hope it's real and hope it's more than a peaking of hormones. But the Christian also says that this invisible God did make Himself visible in a unique miracle called the Incarnation (literally, "becoming flesh," the Son of God coming to Earth). Among the disciples of Jesus, there was a doubter by the name of Thomas, who said, "Unless I see the nail marks in his hands and put my finger where the nails were, and put my hand into his side, I will not believe it" (John 20:25). He did see and touch and hear the resur- rected Jesus, and he did believe.

Another face of atheism in the modern world is the world-view known as *secular humanism*. Two words here: "humanism" and "secular." Humanism, broadly viewed, can either be hostile toward God or accepting of God. Five hundred years ago in the European Renaissance, an interest in understanding humanity gave us Leonardo da Vinci's *Mona Lisa* and his many inventions, as well as Michelangelo's matchless art and sculptures. This kind of humanism also promoted the study of ancient texts, including the Bible in its original languages (Hebrew and Greek), and the printing of books with the new invention by Johann Gutenberg: the printing press. But sometimes "humanism" has meant the rejection of any dehumanizing philosophies or religions, of which there have been many. The Christian faith would agree that we are obliged to respect humanity as a creation of God and to stand against any dehumanizing forces.

There is a kind of humanism that is hostile to belief in God, however. If you say that humanity is the highest and only worthy reality—if you divorce respect for humanity from respect for God, if you make humanism *secular*—then you have something that is trying to stand on its own two feet without the help of God. "Secular" comes from the Latin word *saeculum,* which means "age" or "this age." Secular humanism is a belief that reflects an interest in humanity in an exclusively "this world" sense. As the Greek philosopher Protagoras said, "Man is the measure of all things."

Secular humanism has been expressed and defined in the Humanist Manifestos of 1933 and 1973, and 2003's *Humanism and Its Aspirations: Humanist Manifesto III*, which were signed by highly influential philosophers, authors, economists, political leaders, psychologists and educators. To a large extent, secular humanism shapes the agendas of our schools, government, mass media, courts, and even many churches. Secular humanism says that human freedom is the only sacrosanct principle, and if there are problems, we need to find human solutions instead of looking for salvation from God because religion can only be divisive. If we want peace, we must find common ground in our common humanity.

To believe there is no God is a frightening proposition—not just emotionally, but also logically. Malcolm Muggeridge said that if God is dead, something is going to take His place; it will either be megalomania or erotomania—the drive for power or the drive for pleasure, the clenched fist or the phallus, Hitler or Hugh Hefner. The evidence is not hard to find. Read a book on history. Read any day's newspaper and follow the global stories of the day. A humanism that seeks to liberate the God-created abilities of people, ultimately to the glory of the Creator, elevates us. But a secular humanism that makes humanity the center of and the highest authority in the universe—that makes humans gods—places us in a job for which we are woefully unqualified, as history shows.

Perhaps the most pervasive kind of atheism is what some have called *practical atheism*, the life stance of many who may say they believe in God, but for all intents and purposes, the reality of God never enters their minds, never influences a decision, never shapes a value, never prompts them to worship. Not atheists formally, they might as well be—there is no conscious thought of God or interaction with God. And one might even wonder if practical atheism is more dangerous than dogmatic atheism. Which is more dangerous: to admit you don't believe in God, or to say you do and then absolutely ignore Him? Remember that Jesus reserved His strongest words for those who claimed righteousness but who defined it in their own terms.

Psalm 53:1 says, "The fool says in his heart, 'there is no God.'" This is a picture of practical atheism. This psalm talks about what happens when people just give up seeking God. It says, "God looks down from heaven . . . to see if there are any who understand, any who seek God. Everyone has turned away, they have together become corrupt; there is no one who does good, not even one" (vv. 2-3). In other words, loose yourself from God and you may sense that you are free but only as free as a ship without anchor, without compass, without a harbor—tossed by the wind and waves with no horizon, no ultimate destination, no precious cargo, no purpose that endures beyond the length of your life.

What do those who believe in God have to say in response to atheism?

First, the cosmos itself is evidence of God. Even non-believing astrophysicists today look at the universe and say that it appears that there is design running through it. Now design implies a designer. "The heavens declare the glory of God; the skies proclaim the work of his hands. Day after day they pour forth speech; night after night they display knowledge. . . . Their voice goes out into all the earth, their words to the ends of the world" as it says in Psalm 19:1-4. The cosmos, in other words, is not "all there is or ever was or ever will be." The cosmos is shouting out the truth that it was created. The heavens display knowledge—knowledge of the one true God.

Second, there is the fact that we want to believe. We have these strong spiritual instincts, which are hard to explain if there is no God. How can we even have a concept of God if there is no God? Even the atheist couldn't talk about not believing in God if he did not have the ability to think about God—and where might that ability come from?

Third, our moral sensibilities are evidence of God. Virtually every human society has had a sense of "oughtness" in it—that there are some things we ought to do and other things we ought not. Specific laws vary from one group to the next, but this moral instinct is the thing to notice. Where does it come from? Even if you look at the most basic moral standard—something like "You should not steal my car"— there is no reason why we can say that unless there is a Lawgiver above who has imparted the thing we call values, a sense of right and wrong.

Now these are all logical arguments for the existence of God (you can follow other claims for the existence of God, such as the "cosmological argument" in other books), but there is more to go on than that. As Dietrich Bonhoeffer said, "A God who let us prove his existence would be an idol."[3]

What do we find in the voices of Scripture and, specifically, in the teachings of Jesus? Jesus spent no time arguing for the existence of God. He didn't need to. But that does not mean that Jesus has nothing to say to modern atheism or secular humanism. There is one statement that Jesus made that is a kind of theistic manifesto. It is an explosion of loud truths that describe a personal and all-powerful God. We know it as the Lord's Prayer (see Matt. 6:9-13).

God Is

Our Father in heaven, hallowed be your name . . .

The Lord's Prayer begins simply: "Our Father in heaven, hallowed be your name" (v. 9). Now you could say nothing more than that and have a belief system that fills in the deep cracks and fissures of atheism or materialism. Four truths: There is a God, He is personal and benevolent, He is above and apart from this finite world, and He is great and worthy of adoration. By recommending that the disciples and you and I speak to God, Jesus is saying that you can trust that there really is a Creator who can hear the sound of your voice and who (amazingly!) *wants* to hear your voice. Because this God is called Father, we know Him to be very different from the impersonal cosmic force that some religions think God to be. He is different from the cosmos itself, which He created out of nothing and then shaped as a potter takes his clay and forms it according to the vision in his mind. He is a personal God, which means that He thinks and acts out of His conscious ability to self-will; He creates; and He relates. A Father God has an implicit relationship with what He creates, especially the creatures He calls sons and daughters. This is almost too good to be true. We have not only a Master Designer, but the head of a human family. And, analogous to a good earthly father, He provides what He knows we need, He protects us as His dependents and He guides us as our Master.

God is in heaven, which is not, as some skeptics want to depict in simplistic terms, outer space. Back in 1962, the second Soviet cosmonaut to go into space thought he was making a strong anti-theistic statement when he said, "Some say God is living there [in space]. I was looking around very attentively. But I did not see anyone there. I did not detect angels or gods. . . . I don't believe in God. I believe in man—his strength, his possibilities, his reason."[4] Major Titov thought that he had gone into heaven and found it to be the

empty, dark space it appears to be from Earth, which is a little like a kindergartner living in Arizona taking one step outside the house and declaring, "There is no such thing as
oceans." I wonder if a meteorite had punched a hole in Major
Titov's capsule if even he might have been tempted to pray
to a God he couldn't see.

In 1968, the crew of Apollo 8, whose mission was to be
the first human beings in history to leave the orbit of planet Earth and travel a quarter million miles across the darkness of space and loop around the moon, radioed back to
Earth on Christmas Day the following message from the
Bible's opening words, the account of creation: "In the
beginning God created the heavens and the earth. The earth
was formless and void, and darkness was over the surface of
the deep. And the Spirit of God moved upon the face of the
waters. And God said, 'Let there be light': and there was
light. And God saw the light, and it was good" (Gen. 1:1-4,
NASB). Everyone I have ever talked to who remembered that
broadcast from the moon's orbit was deeply moved by it.
For me, it was a moment when our highest scientific achievement to date was marked by the anchor point of all spiritual truth.

The God who is dwells in all places at all times. He touch-
es our world and so our lives, but as heaven-dweller. He
exists in dimensions beyond our sensible knowledge and
beyond our imagining.

If you believe nothing more than that, then you are
talking to a God who must be "hallowed," which means to
hold in the highest regard, to treat as holy and worthy of
deep reverence. Atheism robs us of reverence. It says that
the highest reality you can point to is yourself, which may

seem like a compliment and a way of having nobility and dignity in life. But it is a bit like standing in a barrel and trying to lift yourself off the ground. If the self is the highest and holiest reality, then you either worship the self or you guess that there is nothing in the universe actually worth being worshiped.

God Wills

Your kingdom come, your will be done . . .

The second part of the Lord's Prayer, this manifesto of theism, says, "Your kingdom come, your will be done on earth as it is in heaven" (v. 10). If you pray that, then you are saying, "I believe God is a ruling king. He is leader over what He has created, He has a plan, and He knows how it all is supposed to work, so that means that He knows how my life is supposed to work.

When I am confused or feel strung out, discouraged or like giving up, He is the Protector and the ruling Sovereign. I want His kingdom to come, for His gracious and generous, wise and right reign in my life, in the life of my family and in my community. Bring it on, God! Tell me what I should do, show me reality. *Your will be done.* Just as in heaven things are right and true and harmonious and orderly, please help me to cooperate with Your will on Earth. Take my own will, which is strong and sometimes wild, which can be over-anxious or overly lethargic, take my conscious center of volition, and bring it alongside Your will. May other people look at my life and say, 'That is obviously what God wants life to be.'"

God Gives

Give us this day our daily bread . . .

Jesus said that we should pray, "Give us this day our daily bread" (v. 11). For people who don't know where their next meal is coming from or who are worried about the loss of their job or the shrinking of their pension, this is a prayer that is felt at the gut level. But even for those who aren't really worried about stocking the pantry and who worry more about too many carbohydrates, this is an apt prayer because of what we are actually saying: "Lord, what I have, You have given; what I do not yet have, I need to receive from You. I do not make grain grow in the field. I don't make the sun shine or the rain fall. I did not construct my digestive system, and I don't control how it works. Thank You, thank You, thank You for Your hearty gifts. I cannot pay You back for what You have given any more than any child can repay his or her mom or dad. I am glad that I can know You and that You Yourself are the greatest hope for generosity and grace in this grabby world." As one nineteenth-century poet said, "The worst moment for the atheist is when he is really thankful and has nobody to thank."

God Forgives

Forgive us our trespasses, as we forgive . . .

"Forgive us our trespasses" (v. 12). Now you can be an atheist and believe in repentance and forgiveness, but they can never amount to anything more than a reconciliation between human beings. That would be a good accomplishment and better than nothing. But there are a couple of major problems. First, how high is the motivation for reconciliation between us and other people? If there is no God, if there is no moral absolute above us and apart from us, why should I go through the work of seeking forgiveness or granting it for that matter? An atheist may argue that reconciliation and peace is a better state of affairs because reducing injury between people or groups is a more desirable way to live. But that is so far removed from the theistic reason for reconciliation that it can hardly be compared. It is the difference between a teenager saying he or she is sorry for carelessly backing over the neighbor's dog in the driveway because "sorry" is a magic word for getting along with other people, and truly grieving that his or her carelessness made the neighbor's children heartbroken.

Another problem with understanding forgiveness apart from God is that we will never find forgiveness for those trespasses that rise above human relationships. We won't find it, because we won't believe we need it. Though in our souls, how we know we need it! If you believe the Lord's Prayer, this theistic manifesto, you will pray, "Forgive me, dear God. Forgive me for being small-minded; forgive me for pettiness in my heart; forgive me for making myself the center of my world and making myself the measure of all things. Forgive me for not aspiring to what is noble." And then what happens? If you believe in God, if you are a true theist and you know that the Son of God gave these words for you to use, then you will find release. That is, after all, what forgiveness is. You are freed from the grip of legal obligation and of your own guilt and shame. But you can only pray that if there is a God whose ear is next to our mouths.

And then there is the follow-on: "as we forgive those who sin against us" (v. 12). The theistic manifesto says this, too: Experiencing the freedom of the release of forgiveness from God goes hand in hand with us doing the same with others. And how could it work any other way?

God Protects

Lead us not into temptation, but deliver us from evil . . .

"Lead us not into temptation, but deliver us from evil" (v. 13). Now a positive belief in God goes hand in hand with certain beliefs about the darker side of spiritual life—realities like temptation and evil. The Christian acknowledges such realities and admits that they are the best explanation for the spiritual and moral catastrophes that happen in life, but the Christian can have hope because of the ability of God to provide protection from temptation and evil. The atheist, on the other hand, has to come up with an entirely different solution. It is almost unbearable to think that we are subject to temptation and evil, and there is no salvation at hand. So the easiest thing to do is to deny it all. Temptation? Why hang on to that old notion that clings to the story of Eden and the forbidden tree? Are we not free creatures? And as long as we're not hurting someone else, who can say we're doing anything wrong or succumbing to some temptation? Crime is a problem, yes. Cruelty, yes. But temptation?

So, too, for the atheist, it is hard to allow that there is evil in the world, because that is a spiritual judgment. To call something evil means describing not merely an illegality but also a crime against heaven and a purposeful, dark, energetic malevolence. To believe that there is evil is to believe in spiritual realities that exist beyond the acts of human beings. So Christians pray, according to the directions of Jesus, "Deliver us from evil," which means, protect us from the ravages of the evil acts of others by keeping us spiritually strong, help us to have faith, be our fortress. It is to say, "Help me to know that You have vanquished the Evil One, that he cannot snatch me from Your hand, that he cannot bury me."

God Rules

Yours is the kingdom, power and glory . . .

And finally, "Yours is the kingdom and the power and the glory" (v. 13). God rules. This means that with a clear perspective on the events of the whole world and of your own life, you can say, "You are the One who is ruling, and Your power is the only power that ultimately matters, and Your glory—Your greatness, Your goodness, Your majesty—is what gives the matters of my life value." It is to define your life in relation to the God who is. This is the black-and-white opposite of what the atheist is doing with life. The atheist or the secular humanist is committed to defining all of life without God: There is no divine interference, but no divine provision either.

And so the prayer concludes, "Forever and ever. Amen" (v. 13). Whenever I pray that final phrase, it strikes me in the face: "forever." All of these statements about God and to God are not intended to be passing sentiments, but eternal convictions. *Forever* commitments. In a university classroom, a debate about theism versus atheism may be a 50-minute experience—and then it's on to geography, mass communications or English 101. But in real life, believing or not believing that there is a God—and that kingdom, power and glory are His special characteristics—may be the difference between a life lived in hope or a life of despair.

Notes

1. Ellen Johnson, "Atheist Families—The Murray O'Hair Family," transcript available at AmericanAtheists.org. http://www.americanatheist.org/conv25/e johnson.html (accessed June 2007).
2. Ibid.
3. Dietrich Bonhoeffer, *No Rusty Swords* (New York: Harper and Row, 1947).
4. Gherman Titov, Soviet cosmonaut, comments at World's Fair, Seattle, Washington, May 6, 1962, as reported by *The Seattle Daily Times*, May 7, 1962, p. 2.

CHAPTER 9

The New Face of Earth Religions

Janet was in most respects a typical 16-year-old girl from the Midwest. A good student, she didn't really fit into any of the cliques in her school, and there was just one other girl and a fellow whom she talked to. Her dad ran a small business and her mom took care of the younger kids at home and worked part-time as a check-out clerk. They belonged to the same church that three generations had, although they didn't attend much more often than Christmas, Easter and the occasional wedding or funeral.

What the family never talked about was the group that Janet had joined a year before. Not a school club, not a church youth group, not a civic organization—this was a Wicca group, a coven. Their numbers were small and they felt persecuted, but that had the effect of pulling them together.

The contours of this story could be told many times over in the United States. Surveys show that there are about 300,000 people in the U.S. (and about a million worldwide) who describe themselves as "Pagans," "Wiccans," or "Druids," although there are other groups that generally ascribe to a neo-pagan approach to life.[1] There are, for example, 30 groups in the state of Wisconsin bearing such names as the "Circle

of the Silver Dragonfly Coven," the "Grove of the Laughing
Oak Coven," the "Re-formed Congregation of the Goddess
International," the "Circle of Solitaires" and the "Coven of
the Unhewn Stone."[2]

While startling to many today, in the days of the early
Christians, pagan religions were the norm. The Christians
were the minority with the startlingly unique belief in an
incarnation of God in the person of Jesus of Nazareth. They
proclaimed Him to be the Lord of heaven and Earth, the
light and life of God, the only hope for salvation in a hopelessly divided world. *Strange . . . very strange,* the mainstream
religionists of the day thought.

There are so many different ideas today of who God is (or
isn't), and how to follow Him (or, some would claim, Her).
There is a search going on for God. A recent poll by the Pew
Internet and American Life Project showed that more people
use the Internet for spiritual purposes than for gambling,
banking, or trading stocks. Three million people a day go
looking for spiritual guidance or information, up 50 percent
from the previous year.[3] And you can find almost any alternative you are looking for on the Internet. You can go to an
interactive Buddhist site, which helps you with breathing and
meditation through an animated candle flame that grows and
diminishes on your screen. You can study the Koran. You can
find a coven in your area or join in a neo-pagan chat group.

Wild variations of religions would not have been strange
to the apostles Peter or Paul. In the days of early Christianity,
the Greco-Roman world was a surging sea of religions, sects,
philosophies, rites and rituals. People could go from worshiping a bull if they belonged to the Mithras cult (very popular among the Roman army) to worshiping the emperor by

burning a pinch of incense at a public shrine to giving an offering to the gods of the city. The early churches had new believers who brought superstition with them into their new faith and who thought that you could still belong to two or three different religions at the same time. Christians grasped that the grace and forgiveness, truth and power they found in Jesus set them in a unique relationship with God. They did not try to mix oil and water.

One modern proponent of earth religions mimicked the chorus of an old gospel song when he wrote, "Give me that *real* old time religion." Going back to mankind's earliest history, there have been religions that either worshiped the earth or believed in spiritual powers associated with the earth.

For example, whoever built Stonehenge in England and similar sites thousands of years ago were probably involved in some sort of ritual of earth and spirit—and very likely worship of the sun—designed to pull in the favor of the gods. So modern neo-pagan groups can be seen using ancient Stonehenge for their own rituals on four special days of the year: the summer and winter solstices, and the spring and fall equinoxes. These are pivotal events of the relationship between Earth and the sun. And if you think the cosmos is the greatest and highest reality, then you might think of the solstices and equinoxes as religious events.

The word "pagan" literally means "something coming from the countryside." Many primal, or earth, religions began with the idea of fertility of the earth. People lived or died depending on whether their crops grew, so they thought they needed the favor of earth, vegetation or rain gods.

These religions are indeed ancient. The Old Testament reports many variations. Baal was the god of fertility (and so

had power over rain, wind and clouds). Ashtoreth was goddess of war and love. And then there was Molech. The worship of Molech was severely condemned by the prophets of
Israel because those who gave obeisance to this god sometimes sacrificed children. The low point came when even the
king of Judah, Ahaz, sacrificed his own sons (see 2 Chron.
28:3). But spiritual revival came for the Israelites during the
reign of the next king, Hezekiah. The task of the prophets
and kings was to reject any god who was a make-believe substitute for the one true God, who was alive and personal and
all-powerful.

In the New Testament era, there was worship of Zeus
and Apollo, gods of power and intellect, and of Dionysus,
god of revelry, and the goddess Artemis, the goddess of earth
and fertility, who appealed to the passionate side of people.
Although by the first century A.D. most people didn't believe
these gods actually existed, they still carried out rites and rituals to make sure that the gods—whoever they might be—
would grant hearty crops and military victories.

Now skip ahead, way ahead, to the twenty-first century.
Earth religions were thought to have died out during the
spread of Christianity in the West, but today a new wave of
interest in the primal has resulted in a rebirth of paganism.
The number of people involved is not large compared to
the major world religions, but interest is growing, especially among young adults. Some talk about their conversions
to paganism, like the enlisted soldier from Mountain View,
California, who wrote in an Internet chat room:

> Hi all. Thanks for supporting us. I was surprised to
> see this posting here. I became a Pagan while in the

Army back in 1988, I was on guard duty in Germany, and the guy I was with was a Pagan, we were alone in the middle of the forest for [several] hours, a great place to talk and learn about it, and ever since then I have considered myself Pagan.

You should have seen the look on the clerk's face when I went to update my personal records and changed my religion from Catholic to Pagan. She looks at me and says, "What does that mean, you worship cows or something?"[4]

Many neo-pagan groups focus on the earth, ascribing to it a spiritual identity and giving it the ancient name of the goddess Gaia. The "Gaia Hypothesis" is the belief that the biosphere of our planet is a living being. The religion usually goes hand in hand with a radical form of feminism and often with radical forms of environmentalism. Care of the earth (a biblical principle) is exaggerated into worship of the earth.

Wicca is a modern form of witchcraft, which seeks to use magical powers to manipulate the classical elements—earth, air, fire and water. Most Wiccans worship the earth in the form of a goddess and a god, representing the complementing polarities seen in nature.

Other modern groups are variations of Druidism, whose roots are in ancient Britain. Modern Druids believe there are many gods and goddesses, and although some believe in a Supreme Deity, they reject any figure of ultimate evil such as the devil. They are wary of technology and are insistent on religious toleration.

So what is the attraction of primal religions? Why would a 16-year-old girl or a sergeant in the Army or a 25-year-old computer programmer risk their reputations and bring on themselves almost certain disdain from others?

First, primal religions offer something new that is actually something old, something ancient. Some people are attracted to that. They like the idea of taking a giant leap out of the modern technological world, a world divided into several large but mutually exclusive religions, and back to the days of fertility rituals and astrological forces. Back to pre-civilization. Back to a time when spells were cast and people believed the earth itself is a spiritual entity.

Neo-pagan religions also are interested in the sub-rational and the ritualistic. It is pre-scientific, pre-philosophy, pre-Hinduism, pre-Buddhism, pre-Jewish, pre-Christian, pre-Muslim. Instead of heady philosophy, it is fleshy ritual.

Neo-pagan religions seek to promote a direct relationship with the earthy, the tangible. Everyone knows that part of living is figuring out how to survive in the environment. Neo-paganism says that this is the main issue in life.

For some people, being a neo-pagan in the modern world is a perfect way to have a countercultural identity. Though the number of neo-pagans is growing, earth religions are still very much out of the mainstream. And primal religions often promote personal autonomy. There is no hierarchy that anyone is beholden to. There are rarely congregational responsibilities of members of covens. There is no dogma, not even a central rite to which adherents are bound. The closest thing Wiccans have to a central creed is the "Rede" (advice, counsel): *An ye harm none, do what ye will.* In other words, you are entirely free to do what you want, as long as it doesn't harm anybody else. (This is a kind of inverse, reactive version of the Golden Rule—which is "Do to others what you would have them to do to you"—stripped down to "Don't do to others what will harm them.") This lack of hierarchical authority is appealing to many followers of neo-pagan religions who are looking for empowerment.

Christians contend that some of the tenets of neo-pagan religion seem to draw power that comes out of darkness, the realm of the satanic in biblical terms. What about this?

In the Scriptures, two seemingly conflicting viewpoints about pagan gods are set forth. First, the other gods are false gods and non-existent gods. That is the point of the dramatic encounter between the prophet Elijah and the prophets of Baal on Mt. Carmel where Elijah challenges the worshipers of Baal to implore their god to lick up their sacrifice with fire. Nothing happens. No fire, no smoke, no god. Then Elijah asks the Lord to take his sacrifice, and fire descends from heaven (see 1 Kings 18:16-46).

This story shows that Baal was nullified because he was shown to be an invention of people's imaginations. This theme was picked up by other prophets, as recorded in the Bible. Isaiah ridiculed false gods by saying a man cuts down a tree, uses some of it as firewood to warm himself and bake his bread, and "he also fashions a god and worships it" (44:15). And the apostle Paul said in 1 Corinthians 8 "that an idol is nothing at all in the world . . . there is no God but one. For even if there are so-called gods . . . yet for us there is but one God" (vv. 4-6).

On the other hand, the Bible also presents us with the viewpoint that the false gods may have some reality after all. The apostle Paul says in 1 Corinthians 10:20 that the sacrifices of pagans are offered to demons. The New Testament without ambiguity asserts that one of the root causes of evil in the world are the unseen powers of evil, that Satan and demons are real (see Eph. 6:10-18).

How can we reconcile these two viewpoints? By realizing that they can both be true. People can make up spiritual beliefs, but they can also be deceived and energized by very real, evil spirits.

There are many stories from different parts of the world that repeat what we find in the Bible about the power of God and the power of the demonic clashing.

A few years ago I traveled with some friends to the remote villages of southern Ethiopia. The small plane we were in traversed the sharp ridges of mountains that looked like they were covered in green felt that then dropped away to vast expanses of desert brush. We flew over rivers where hundreds of flamingos suddenly broke into flight, splotches of pink flowing in their own kind of river. In the deep south, far away from civilization, we landed on a dusty strip—but only after the pilot buzzed the red patch of dirt to chase a couple of cows and goats off of it. Pictures of villagers like the ones we met appeared on the pages of *National Geographic* in years past, showing off the lip disks that progressively stretch the lips into large protruding bills. Many of the women wore rings of metal all up their necks, some with a post off the front end. (I was told the post was used by husbands as they beat their wives.)

In a village like that, you see either fear etched in people's faces or a vacant, emotionless, flat expression. The local witch doctors exercise domination and control, and people live in fear of spells cast and of the spirits of dead villagers haunting the village. But we also saw in that same village an entirely different look in the faces of the Jesus believers. They were free and believed themselves to be forgiven. Their faces were bright and responsive. They had withdrawn themselves from the domination of witchdoctors. They walked with purposeful strides, so unlike the woman I passed on the path whose face was drained and who dragged her legs. The gods of her village had done nothing for her but put her in a state of fear, expecting the worst.

The face of neo-paganism is different in a modern American mall. One of my friends told me of an encounter he had in a local bookstore. As he and his daughter waited in line to be checked out, just ahead of him was a 16- or 17-year-old girl dressed very darkly, with pale makeup, spiked hair and wearing rough, spiked jewelry and chains. He noticed that she had laid a couple of books on sorcery and witchcraft on the counter. Then he noticed a band on her arm with the letters W-W-J-D. My friend, whose first reaction was to hold back, ventured to make conversation, asking the girl about the band on her arm. She said she got it from a friend and that the letters stood for "What would Jesus do?" He then felt free to simply tell her that the things she was hoping to find in those books would turn out to be a big disappointment, whereas she could find the love of God in Jesus, as her bracelet indicated. The cashier asked for the money, the girl paid and disappeared with her books, and the man and his daughter took a moment to pray for her in the mall.

One of the most important discussions Jesus ever had with His disciples, and a true turning point in His ministry, happened in the back country of Palestine. It was not in Jerusalem, not in Galilee, not in Samaria. One day Jesus and His disciples were in the far north at the foot of great Mount

Hermon, the only snow-capped mountain in the region. This beautiful place was Caesarea Philippi, and it was a long way from home.

The setting was pagan Syria. We aren't told exactly why Jesus took His disciples to this remote place, but we do know they were outside their normal element. Here at the base of Mount Hermon were flowing springs and pools. It was lush and fertile, and for generations this place of water and life was the site of shrines to Baal and to the Roman god Pan.

Now Jesus and His disciples weren't there to do anything about paganism. But it was the setting for an encounter with truth, a defining moment for the followers of Jesus.

"Who do people say I am?" asked Jesus (Mark 8:27; see also Matt. 16:13). Probably most of the disciples knew that that was the real issue of the day. It wasn't about the specific teachings Jesus was giving, and it wasn't about a new organization Jesus was talking about founding with His disciples. Jesus had not been training His followers to begin a new religion. He came into the world, the eternal Son of God, the Lord of the universe, in order to rescue human beings from the grip of their sins, to free them from the oppression of the Evil One, to make them alive from within. But it all hinges on who He is. Five hundred years before Christ, Buddha tried to point away from himself. Six hundred years after Christ, Muhammad in Arabia did not make his personal identity the main issue.

But with Jesus it was different. When Jesus asked, "Who do people say I am?" He was not asking what the polls were saying or trying to figure out what His approval rating was. He wanted to get out in the open, right then and there, who was getting it and who wasn't. Whether modern people liked it or not, Jesus forced an issue. He claimed to be the Messiah and the Son of God sent from heaven. Able to forgive people their sins. Worthy of the worship of people who went down on their knees before Him.

So who was getting it? The disciples recounted the main speculations of the day: Jesus must be one of the prophets, maybe even someone come back to life, like Elijah or John the Baptist.

And then Jesus turned the question on the disciples themselves, which was what Jesus always did. He was not interested in collations of public opinion about Him. What He wanted to know was, "What about you?" As was often the case, Peter was the lead voice of the disciples. And on this day, he got it.

"You are the Christ, the Son of the living God" (Matt. 16:16; Mark 8:29). There, it was said, right in the backyard of Baal and Pan. Out in the world of the *paganos*, where faith is either related to mother earth or to the heavens.

The *Christos,* which in Hebrew is *Messiach*, Messiah. Anointed One. A greater King than David, who was unique in the line of kings in the Old Testament. Unique in how he was anointed one day by the prophet Samuel (see 1 Sam. 16:1-13). Anointed to carry out God's unique plan. And after David, the prophets pointed ahead to one who would come some day out of the lineage of David. "Watch that family line," they said, "because one day God's salvation for all mankind will appear—right there."

Son of the living God. There are so many supposed gods. But how many even claim to be *alive*—that is, active and engaged in this world that was fashioned like a great work of art. Alive in interacting with human beings whom He created. Alive to their hurts, to their needs. Alive in responding to their failures. Gaia, the earth goddess, is not alive in that way. The earth lives, yes, but only because the Creator conceived of it and brought out of the darkness and void both the heavens and the earth. He made the vast blue oceans and the lush green forests. Beautiful and ordered are not just the way the heavens and the earth are; it is the way God intended them to be. God is not the sun, and He is not the seasons. He knows of solstices and equinoxes, but the sun runs its course like a chariot across the sky because God put it all together.

Baal was not alive. In the days when King Ahab of Israel had welcomed worship of Baal and there were 450 Baal priests in Israel itself, the prophet Elijah challenged the priests of Baal on Mount Carmel. The great revelation of the day was that when they called fire down upon the wood and sacrifice, there was only silence. Elijah taunted them all: "Surely he is a god! Perhaps he is deep in thought, or busy, or traveling. Maybe he is sleeping and must be awakened" (1 Kings 18:27). Still, silence. "Baal" is just a word.

You can go to Stonehenge on the autumnal equinox to meditate or perform a rite, but how can you expect to meet the living God in lifeless rock formations? Millions of people believe that we can know the living God through the vibrant life and person of Jesus. And to comprehend that Jesus is the Messiah, the Son of the living God, is ultimately a revelation from God the Father in heaven.

To be a Christian does not mean that you acquiesce to a religion imposed on you by birth or coercion. It doesn't even mean that you sign up with a religious alternative that seems to have an impressive balance of pros and cons. To be a Christian means that your eyes are opened one day to the brilliant light of God's truth: You see that Jesus is the way of reconciliation with God, the source of rock-solid truth and the right object of your adoration and worship. It is not only Peter the fisherman who received the revelation from the Father but also everyone who later becomes a true disciple of Jesus. And there are consequences.

After Peter's statement "You are the Christ, the Son of the living God," Jesus used a play on the words "Peter" (*Petros*) and "rock" (*petra*): "On this rock I will build my church" (Matt. 16:18) was Jesus' way of saying that this confessing believer, enlightened by God, vocal in his belief and clear in his understanding, was the building material that He would use to build a mighty thing called the Church. And when we make a similar profession about Jesus, we become part of the Church's foundation.

This thing called Church is not merely a religion. It is not a school of philosophy. And it is not only a spiritual practice. It is a new community. Church is a living body of people, a communion of saints. It flows across cultural lines; it moves with ease from one century to the next. Christ's Church is the answer for lonely and disenfranchised people living in impoverished third-world countries and for disconnected people living in sophisticated technological metropolises.

And there is nothing that will stop it. Jesus said He would build it. The power of Hades—the power of death—can't stop it any more than it could hold Jesus' body in perfumed cloths in a tomb. There is thus no reason for the Christian to be afraid of paganism, neo-paganism or any -ism that offers people a different kind of salvation by a different kind of god. Rather, the life and love of the people of God are a continually flowing gift of God to any person.

Now, it is the calling and privilege of the believing follower of Jesus, like Peter, to open the door that swings widely into God's household by proclaiming with clarity and
grace the offer of forgiveness in Jesus.

Peter could take no credit for anything. He knew what
he knew by faith and because the living God had opened his
eyes to the truth. It's not that he was better than anybody
else or smarter than anyone else. And so the Christian today
is not saying, "I'm smarter, I'm better, I've got a better quality religion." He or she is saying, "Blessed. How blessed I am
that among so many gods, the one true God has shined His
light in such a way that billions of people can know Him as
the way, the truth and the life."

Jesus Himself forced the issue of what we are to make of
Him. In his classic work *Mere Christianity*, C. S. Lewis dispos-
es of the idea that Jesus was simply a great moral teacher:

A man who was merely a man and said the sort of
things Jesus said would not be a great moral teacher.
He would either be a lunatic—on the level with the
man who says he is a poached egg—or else he would
be the Devil of Hell. You must make your choice.
Either this man was, and is, the Son of God; or else a
madman or something worse. You can shut Him up
for a fool, you can spit at Him and kill Him as a
demon; or you can fall at His feet and call Him Lord
and God. But let us not come with any patronizing
nonsense about His being a great human teacher. He
has not left that open to us. He did not intend to.[5]

Notes

1. "The American Religious Identification Survey," conducted by The City University of New York, 2001.
2. "Groups and Organizations," Wisconsin Spirit Pathways online. http://www.spiritpathways.com/groups.html (accessed June 2007).
3. Lynn Schofield Clark and Stewart Hoover, "Faith Online: 64% of Wired Americans Have Used the Internet for Spiritual or Religious Purposes," Pew Internet and American Life Project. http://www.pewinternet.org/PPF/r/126/report_display.asp (accessed June 2007).
4. From a posting on the Paganism discussion board at Beliefnet.com dated October 24, 2001. http://www.beliefnet.com/boards/message_list.asp?discussionID=90929 (accessed June 2007).
5. C. S. Lewis, *Mere Christianity* (New York: Touchstone, 1996), p. 56.

CHAPTER 10

Many Religions, One River?

Deep in the Himalaya mountains, in a glacier at 25,446 feet, is an ice cave whose melting waters course down the mountain and form the beginnings of the great Ganges River, which winds some 1,560 miles through one of the world's most densely populated regions and most fertile plains. In Hindu mythology, Ganges is one of the two goddess daughters of the mountain god Himalaya.

The river has mystical meaning for the people who have lived for millennia along its banks. It is believed that bathing in this river is a means of washing away one's sins, and water from the river is used in many religious rituals. Good fortune comes to those who can drink from the waters of the Ganges an hour before death, it is believed, and many Hindus seek to be cremated and have their ashes scattered over its surface.

This practice, along with the introduction of sewage and industrial waste into the river, has made it dangerously polluted. To drink from the Ganges is regarded as a spiritually significant act, but it is a risk to one's physical body.

There have been times in history when people have held to a religion that is an accumulating combination of many diverse mythological, cultural and spiritual currents. Like a river picking up ever greater volume by the influx of streams and tributaries, this kind of religious experience is a wide

and varied flow of sometimes wildly different theological
ideas, spiritual practices, forms of devotion, mythology and
philosophy. Some view this as a positive thing, while others
find the amalgam a mess.

Such is the case with one of the oldest religions in the
world, Hinduism, whose name doesn't come from that of
any founder or of a theological idea but from geography.
"Hindu" comes from the Sanskrit word *sindhu,* which simply
means "river." Today there are approximately one billion
Hindus worldwide, who live mostly in India, East Africa,
South Africa, Southeast Asia, the West Indies and England.

For more than 4,000 years, the cultural and religious
ideas of the Indus Valley have flowed together into a cultural stream that has continued to pick up more ideas and
more gods right up to the present time. Hinduism embraces
millions of deities, although, paradoxically, it also holds that
there is only one god.

It is extraordinarily difficult for the typical Westerner to
understand the complexities and seeming contradictions of
Hinduism. There are millions of gods but one God. There
are widely diverse scriptures. There is poetic mythology like
the *Bhagavad Gita* (which means "song of the lord") that is
associated with Krishna, sacrificial rituals, university-level
philosophy and the political ethics of Mahatma Gandhi. Of
course, the Hindu may say some of the same things about
Christianity, which worldwide has many different group-
ings, devotional practices and philosophical streams.

If we do some work in trying to understand the spiritual search represented in Hinduism, we will better comprehend that spiritual longing we all have, and we will better
understand what we ourselves believe.

The beliefs of Hinduism begin with a concept of God, called Brahman. The search for Brahman is at its heart. Brahman is eternal being, the ultimate reality. Though in some phases of Hinduism God is seen as personal, most of the time God is more of an "it" than a "who." Everything that exists is part of Brahman, and Brahman infuses everything that exists. This is a view known as *pantheism*, which is one of three or four main ways human beings have thought of God throughout history. There really aren't that many alternatives. Either there is no God (atheism), there is an identifiable personal God (theism), there are numerous gods (polytheism), or God is everything (pantheism).

Now, here is where we begin to encounter a river of different ideas. Hinduism sometimes seems theistic, sometimes polytheistic and sometimes pantheistic, all of which seem to be mutually exclusive. But this is one of the main features of Hinduism. Its adherents believe it to be a universal religion precisely because all these different tributaries flow in, regardless of their seeming contradiction. And in the modern world where many people want to make their entire creed "You believe what you believe and I'll believe what I believe; what is true for me must be true and what is true for you must also be true," this Eastern outlook is highly attractive.

Here is the next step. Brahman is eternal being and reality itself. But what we know and experience as the physical world around us is an illusion, a kind of dream. The world as we know it as human beings—the world of time and space and individual personality—is not reality. Our goal, Hinduism says, is to raise the level of our consciousness so that we can perceive the eternal, leaving behind the world of touch and taste and smell and sight and sound.

Our perception of ourselves as individual, isolated creatures, our inner self, is known as *atman*. The spiritual goal of
Hinduism is for the limited inner self (*atman*) to realize that
it is part of a great universal being, which is God. What we
know as personhood or self gradually fades away as we go
through successive reincarnations in life until we finally are
merged with God, when *atman* has become Brahman.

I'm sure that we have all met someone along the way
who thought reincarnation makes a lot of sense. I remember when I was a teenager, hearing about Eastern religions
and how they presented intriguing ideas about the afterlife,
like reincarnation. And there was a certain attractiveness
about it.

Why? Well, think about it. Some people are not thrilled
with the idea that when you die, the best you can hope for
is some kind of nondescript heaven where you end up sitting on a cloud, wearing the most unimaginative wardrobe
(some kind of white gown) and listening to harp music, not
for 10 years, not for 1,000 years, but for eternity. (This is, of
course, a terrible and unbiblical view of heaven and the
afterlife, which the Bible describes instead as a newly created heaven and Earth, vital and more alive than anything we
experience in this world, the fulfillment of the very best we
have in this world.)

To some, the idea of being reincarnated, coming back to
good old Earth, your familiar stomping grounds, sounds
far better. And even if you're reincarnated as a dog instead
of a human being, perhaps your karma will have been good
enough to warrant your ending up in a nice home with
pampering owners. At least you'll still have good old Earth
you're familiar with.

The practices of Hinduism are designed to assist the individual in raising his or her consciousness beyond the self. Participating in rituals associated with the shrines of deities and their statues is one way to raise one's consciousness. And then there is meditation. In the 1960s in the United States, the teachings of Maharishi Mahesh Yogi became popular. His Transcendental Meditation invited people to have a soul-cleansing and mind-expanding experience by meditating a few minutes each day on a simple phrase or word, a mantra. The goal of such meditation is to empty the mind, to abandon normal human consciousness so that the self fades into the eternal being.

This, by the way, is the main difference between Eastern meditation and Jewish or Christian meditation, for which the goal is not to empty the mind but to fill it by the conscious pondering of biblical truth and significant imagery. The perfect model is Israel's king and singer of songs, David, whose psalms are an invitation to be joined to God by intentional contemplation of and meditation on His goodness and greatness.

Transcendental Meditation was just one of many Western experiments with Hinduism. At about that same time, many used psychedelic drugs as a way to leave the conscious mind behind and be raised to a higher level of consciousness. But hashish and LSD didn't deliver what was promised, and now hard-drug users don't talk anymore about finding God in a drug-induced state. They are more likely to admit they are seeking simple escape. One drug survivor, actress Carrie Fisher (best known as Princess Leia in the *Star Wars* series) said, "I was seeking mind expansion and pain reduction, but what I ended up with was pain expansion and mind reduction."[1]

Another Western experiment with Hinduism was in the Hare Krishna sect. In the 1960s and '70s, young people started showing up on street corners and in airports, passing out literature, wearing chiffon robes and sporting heads shaved except for a ponytail coming off the back.

The myth of Krishna is beloved in Hinduism. As the eighth incarnation of the god Vishnu, Krishna became the Supreme Person and the highest deity. The legends about Krishna vary, but he is generally held to be a heroic warrior and teacher. His story is told in the poem the *Bhagavad Gita*.

When I was in high school and a new believer, one day I went with a friend who was going to buy a guitar. I picked up one of these things, and though I didn't know anything about how to play it, I walked out with a guitar that day, too. I picked out a nice big one that had 12 strings on it. *If 6 is good, wouldn't 12 be twice as good?* I thought. The next day, reality hit as I realized tuning 12 strings was twice as laborious as tuning 6 and that you needed the fingers of a gorilla to get so many strings pressed against the frets. But oh, did that guitar ring! And, as everybody knew, girls love guys with guitars.

I joined a church group that toured different churches, leading worship services, and I played that thing. It even helped me get the attention of a teenage girl in a church in Sister Bay, Wisconsin, who would later become my wife.

One of the songs that we really liked to play back then was the George Harrison tune "My Sweet Lord" (which I think was played on a 12-string). *What a great song to praise Jesus Christ, Lord of heaven and Earth,* we thought.

We were shocked the day that we realized, however, that the "Lord" the former Beatle was admiring was the Hindu Krishna; and when you listen to the recording carefully, you can hear the words "Krishna, Krishna" in the background. Here we were, singing a song dedicated to Krishna in churches (without backup singers adding the "Krishna, Krishna"). Now if you hold to a Ganges River view of religion, what could be better than letting worship of Jesus and worship of Krishna flow right into each other? But that, of course, was not our intent.

And then there was the night that the Hare Krishna devotee showed up at a youth meeting. When I was in high school, one of the things we did on Sunday evenings was to gather out in the countryside outside Sturgeon Bay, Wisconsin, at a small abandoned country church. It was a small white clapboard building with paint chipping off the exterior and a musty smell inside. Candles were necessary for lack of electricity, and they took the mustiness out of the air.

The 20 or 30 of us who gathered every Sunday night spent a couple of hours singing, reading Scripture, sharing thoughts about Scripture and what God was doing in our lives—just a really great time. One night one of the fellows brought along a friend who rather stood out with the chiffon robe he was wearing and the way his head was shaven all except for a small ponytail in back. At one point in the meeting, the fellow who invited him introduced him and told all of us that we were going to have the opportunity to learn a new kind of praying—a chanting way of praying, whereupon he invited the bald-headed one to address the group. As he began to speak, I knew (even though my own faith was rather undeveloped at the time) that there was something of a spiritual clash in all this, so I stood up (or, I should say, I suddenly realized I was standing, as if I didn't make a conscious choice in the matter), and I objected, telling the group that if we were engaged with the Spirit of God in worship, there was no way that we could or should be involved with any other spirits. The Krishna follower stiffened. And then he asked me and the group this amazing question: "But how will you know what an apple tastes like, unless you take a bite?"

I thought, *Somehow . . . that sounds strangely familiar.* Then it came to me. I suggested that that was the line of thinking that Adam and Eve had taken in the Garden, whereupon the bald fellow and the friend who brought him abruptly departed the church.

Now that young guy was, for his own reasons, attracted to Eastern religion. He wasn't a visiting foreign exchange student from New Delhi; he was a student at the local high school who was on a search for substantive spiritual meaning—a spiritual life that would make a difference. I had to admire his commitment—wearing those clothes, shaving his head, handing out literature. This wasn't San Francisco, after all. It was Door County, Wisconsin, where the winters make long icicles outside your windows and make time stand still, where things change very slowly (and when they do, you assume there must be something wrong), where you know all the locals and whether they're Baptists or Lutherans or Catholics or Moravians. Yet this was a time of real spiritual searching, a spiritual revival. Those of us meeting in that little church just wanted to find a light-filled path in a cynical era.

In trying to understand Hinduism, any honest person living in the West should admit that it is just plain difficult, and over-simplifications should be avoided. We do always learn something by asking, What is the appeal? What is the spiritual dynamic being expressed in Hinduism? And why has there been a keen interest in places like universities to merge East and West?

First, Hinduism is keen on the idea of being a universal religion. Christianity claims the same thing by saying that Jesus Christ is the Savior for the whole world. But what Hinduism means by universal religion is the assumption that all religions are moving toward the same goal and can thus all be true at the same time. Hindus are simply not concerned about apparent contradictions between different religions. These may be problems of logic, strictly speaking, but who is to say that we have to have logical answers to everything? Which leads us to the next point.

Another appealing aspect of Hinduism is the experience of the mystical. The interest in Eastern religions shown by many Westerners has been, in part, a desire to get out of the bondage of modern scientific materialism and naturalism that said that the only reality is the physical universe. Modernism seems to say, "This world is a test tube, and you are a collection of chemicals." But we know better than that. We know that there is a great spiritual universe out there that includes mysteries beyond our imaginings. Christianity has always said that (the apostle Paul wrote many times about the mystery of Christ); but in the modern world, Christians themselves have been guilty of taking the mystery out of the faith, of turning it into a formula or a list of points on paper. When some turn to Hinduism and other Eastern religions, they are probably convinced that Christianity had no mystery to offer. They are wrong, and Christians are often to blame for representing their faith as a house of sticks.

Some have found a theory of salvation in Hinduism that seems to make sense. Life in this world, so filled with contradictions, so full of pain and pleasure, is perhaps an illusion, a gigantic shadow cast on a wall. But if we can find a world of pure spirit, then we will be able to move beyond the stresses and strains of this life.

And for some, the release of the mind through the techniques of meditation has sounded very appealing. Maybe just emptying the mind of all the tensions and confusion is a better alternative than trying to put positive thoughts in. If a guru gives us permission to release all, to be cleared and emptied of all, maybe that's the best we can hope for.

These are some of the reasons for the appeal of Eastern mystical religions. But many who travel to the Indian subcontinent find a bewildering mix of attraction and repulsion. There is the mystery and intrigue, yes, and a sense of connection with the ancient. But the scene at altars and temples of ghastly-looking idols, the sweetish stench of the smoldering offerings, the proliferation of thousands of deities, the squalor in the streets where cows and other animals wander aimlessly—leave many uninitiated confused and repelled. These gods offer the drama of fear and punishment, mockery and cruelty. They offer no grace, no forgiveness. They preside stoically over death and decay, spread like ashes on the sewage-clogged Ganges, with no pity or compassion.

One Christian text that offers a starkly different perspective on life comes from the first epistle of John in the New Testament Scriptures. In the world of the New Testament, there was an abundance of religious alternatives, some of them syncretic, combining elements of this and that religion. (Syncretism is the attempt to produce an amalgam of different religions on the assumption that every one has elements of truth, and the best thing to do is pick and choose the constituent elements to make up a customized religion.) But John makes clear that there is a specificity of truth and a personality behind it:

> Everyone who believes that Jesus is the Christ has become a child of God. And everyone who loves the Father loves his children, too. We know we love God's children if we love God and obey his commandments. Loving God means keeping his commandments, and his commandments are not burdensome. For every child of God defeats this evil world, and we achieve this victory through our faith. And who can win this battle against the world? Only those who believe that Jesus is the Son of God.
>
> And Jesus Christ was revealed as God's Son by his baptism in water and by shedding his blood on the cross—not by water only, but by water and blood. And the Spirit, who is truth, confirms it with his testimony. So we have these three witnesses—the Spirit, the water, and the blood—and all three agree. Since we believe human testimony, surely we can believe the greater testimony that comes from God. And God has testified about his Son. All who believe in the Son of God know in their hearts that this testimony is true. Those who don't believe this are actually calling God a liar because they don't believe what God has testified about his Son.
>
> And this is what God has testified: He has given us eternal life, and this life is in his Son. Whoever has the Son has life; whoever does not have God's Son does not have life.

I have written this to you who believe in the name of the Son of God, so that you may know you have eternal life. And we are confident that he hears us whenever we ask for anything that pleases him. . . .

And we know that the Son of God has come, and he has given us understanding so that we can know the true God. And now we live in fellowship with the true God because we live in fellowship with his Son, Jesus Christ. He is the only true God, and he is eternal life.

Dear children, keep away from anything that might take God's place in your hearts (1 John 5, *NLT*).

The punch line of this text is at the end: "He is the only true God . . . Keep away from anything that might take God's place in your hearts" (literally, "idols").

If we were to ask, *What is it that can help us overcome the great enemies in our lives—the fear of loneliness, disease and death, the temptations of the Evil One, the flaws of our own character—that cause us to fail?*, the New Testament's answer would be *faith*. And the way you gain a vital faith is by a spiritual birth: "Everyone who believes that Jesus is the Christ is a child of God." In other words, coming to know the Father in heaven, through the Christ, is to come alive. Not reincarnation, but a brand-new start that does not need to wait until we die. Unlike reincarnation, this new birth is always a promotion—there is never a time when God says, "I'll give you a new start, but you'll have to go back to square one as a dog or a cockroach instead of a human." Karma does not determine whether we can enter God's family; God does.

As members of this family, we are the objects of God's love and are subject to His command that we love others. For some people, the first part sounds fine, but the second part is a challenge and sounds like an obligatory condition. But the networking of love (God loves us, we love God, God love others, we love others, too, including our enemies) is simply the nature of love. John says that keeping God's commandments "are not burdensome" (1 John 5:3, *NLT*).

My kids are now turning into young adults, and my wife and I have told them this many times. Our expectations of them are not difficult or burdensome. There is work involved (with school, with the house, with the needs of others around), but this is what we're made for. Families aren't designed to just sit around. Don't work and you'll atrophy.

Some people in the West go shopping at the Hindu supermarket, picking and choosing ideas that amount to a religion that has the least amount of obligations—and if there are no obligations, all the better. Besides ignoring Hinduism's fundamental concept of personal responsibility—one's karma is directly related to one's actions—how satisfying can that kind of spiritual life be? What if your teacher had no expectations, or your coach or your parent? Duty gives us dignity. At the end of your life, your concern should not be how comfortable you made yourself but whether you made a difference in the lives of others, that you somehow left things better than you found them.

This kind of faith is the way to victory in life—a pretty bold statement. "For every child of God defeats this evil world by trusting Christ to give the victory. And the ones who win this battle against the world are the ones who believe that Jesus is the Son of God" (1 John 5:4-5, *NLT*).

This is not a battle of religions, and I hope the reader will understand that in these chapters that look at religious alternatives. The point is not to take Christianity into a crusade against other religions—which would be to ignore the real enemies of the human race: "For we are not fighting against people made of flesh and blood, but against the evil rulers and authorities of the unseen world, against those mighty powers of darkness who rule this world, and against wicked spirits in the heavenly places" (Eph. 6:12, *NLT*). No religion has ever won true converts by force. In the Christian gospel, the battle lines are not drawn between people ("flesh and blood") but between the good power of God and the power of the Evil One, which is sometimes manifested in the actions of others.

The Christian is not saying to people of other religions, "I am a better person than you. I am smarter than you." The Christian says, rather, "I have been propelled into believing that Jesus is the Son of God. And I have found that this faith, this living connection with the life of God Himself and being swept into His family, has helped me overcome the world. Not that I don't experience pain and disappointment. Not that I don't fail. But I know, I truly know, that no matter what happens in my life, God is with me—the Father who provides and protects, and Jesus who forgives, and the Holy Spirit who guides and empowers—and so I know nobody can really make me a victim." The Christian says, "I have evidence that this is more than wishful thinking. I want to believe all this, and I have good reason to believe it."

As 1 John 5:6 says, God has made available the testimony of the Spirit, which is the voice of God speaking directly to the human spirit. This voice has a ring of truth to it, and the conviction becomes more and more solid and more and more refined. It is hard to explain because it is beyond explanation. But as believers launch a whole new relationship with God, what they first learned from the testimony of the Spirit is born out to be true.

I grew up in a Christian tradition, but faith really came alive for me when I was 17 years old. I was not expecting to be confronted by the Spirit of God. My mother asked me on a Saturday if I would run my sister's sleeping bag over to her (she was attending a youth retreat at our church), because she had forgotten it. Now I knew that there was a girl at that retreat that I was interested in, so I happily agreed, and my mother probably thought I was just the best kid for being so willing to help.

I marched into the church basement as the 20 or so high school kids were sitting in on a session being led by some college students from another church in Minnesota. I didn't know anything about retreats, nothing about spiritual renewal events, so I was curious and ended up staying the whole day. These college students, fervent believers, were engaged in substantive discussions about God and life, about history and the future. It was not like anything I had heard before. And they were just college students. They led worship sessions with their guitars, read from their worn Bibles and passed out books about faith that they were extremely enthused about. Most striking, however, is that they showed an interest in *me*. They actually engaged *me* in real and personal talk. It was the first time I remember a near-peer drawing me into a spiritual discussion. They really cared. They looked me in the eye and saw a person there. And I sensed they didn't do so because they had to but because they wanted to.

I went home and got my sleeping bag to bring back to the church.

By the time the weekend was over, concluding with a worship service that these guest college students led, I felt like something strange was happening in me. Nobody imposed it on me. Nobody recruited me or asked me to sign up for anything. On Monday and Tuesday and on into the week, I carried about with me a sense that I can only describe as "God is real. God *really* is real." It wasn't much more than that. But I did notice that, without choosing to, I all of a sudden stopped swearing. I asked about when the local group was going to meet again, and I went. I tried to write an essay in which I explained how Christianity and Hinduism and Buddhism and all the rest could be blended into one. I was darting about. I was curious. I was caught.

That was also about the time I met Ingrid, a high schooler like me at the time, who had a very mature faith for her young age. We got into hours-long discussions about God and Scripture and how it all added up. More and more pieces fell into place. The ring of truth was getting louder.

I think that is one way the testimony of the Spirit works. God uses whatever means He chooses to get our attention, anchor the heart, capture the mind. You know God is real, and you know that there is a universe of things about God and the rest of reality that you are about to explore. It is like hiking in a mountain crevasse and suddenly breaking out into a wide open valley.

The other evidences mentioned in 1 John 5:6 are "the testimonies of water and blood," which are most likely references to the baptism and crucifixion of Jesus. Both were public events. Both were landmark moments in the minds of the witnesses. When Jesus went down into the Jordan River, it was not to wash away His sin. This was not the Ganges River, the convergence of innumerable religious streams into one mystical flow, originating in ice caves and ending in a wide, polluted delta. Jesus entered the Jordan River after John the Baptist hesitated; and the people there saw visible signs of the Spirit, who descended like a dove from heaven, and heard that most decisive voice from heaven: "This is my Son, whom I love; with him I am well pleased" (Matt. 3:17). Overwhelming. An absolutely overwhelming testimony.

The same thing was true of the crucifixion. With Jesus' final words, "It is finished" (John 19:30), there was no light from heaven but a foreboding darkness. A Roman soldier understood the testimony and said, "Surely he was the Son of God!" (Matt. 27:54; see also Mark 15:39).

Now testimonies that come from credible people who say and (more important) demonstrate that God is real and who have found forgiveness and purpose in Christ are well and good. But John's higher appeal is to the divine testimony: "Since we believe human testimony, surely we can believe the testimony that comes from God . . . And this is what God has testified: He has given us eternal life, and this life is in his Son" (1 John 5:9,11)

Christian faith says, "God has given. God has given. And then He has given more. I believe what I believe because it has dropped right in front of me. It is a gift beyond compare: eternal life. Life beyond disease and death, life even while I'm still in this body that has an eternal quality to it, that allows me to be more than an animal and more than a collector of goods. God has given eternal life, and it comes through this one clear, conspicuous, controversial figure: Jesus of Nazareth, Jesus the eternal Son of God. And this gives me a confidence that over-arches every other confidence or doubt I have in my life."

At the end of this text, John builds to a crescendo: He has written these things "so that you may know [with certainty] you have eternal life." We can know that God listens to us, that He protects us from sin, that we are children of God, that God gives understanding. And we know that the one thing we have to do is avoid idolatry—anything that would take the place of God in our lives.

"Keep yourselves from anything that might take God's place in your hearts" is John's way of saying one last time, in the simplest and clearest terms, "Whatever you do, *whatever* you do, don't invent any other gods. Don't be allured by invented gods. Don't even invent your beliefs." Faith is only as good and true as it is received. If, among so many gods, there is a true God, then our search for that God is the most important thing we will ever do in life. It is, in fact, a matter of life or death.

Note

1. Carrie Fisher, *Postcards from the Edge* (New York: Pocket Books, 2002).

CHAPTER 11

Jesus and Muhammad

Chuck Colson, founder of Prison Fellowship and heard around the world on his daily radio broadcast *BreakPoint*, relates the following anecdote: A group of women gathered at the Old Country buffet of Boston at the shopping mall. They laughed and chatted as they enjoyed the roast beef and ice-cream sundaes. They could be any group of young moms and college students enjoying a night out. But they're not. These women are recent converts to Islam, celebrating the end of Ramadan. This symbolizes a curious new phenomenon in the wake of September 11: a surge of Islamic conversions. "I said the testimony, and poof, I was a Muslim," said one, a University of Massachusetts theater major. And she added, "I used to feel something was wrong with me because I couldn't grasp the concept of God. Now I finally had peace of heart."[1]

Universities are now in a bidding war for Islamic experts. Every government in the world is sizing up security risks related to extremist Muslim groups, while also trying to figure out how to structure communities that have a blend of Christian, Jewish and Muslim populations, among others.

The story of Islam begins, of course, with the life of the prophet Muhammad, who lived 600 years after Jesus and who wrote the Koran, which means "recitation." Today one

billion Muslims live in almost every country in the world
and believe that this recitation of Allah is the guiding force
of their lives.

Life was hard in the deserts of Arabia in A.D. 600. Blood
feuds, gambling, drunkenness and general chaos ruled. Muhammad, who was in the caravan business, had a disgust for
the times in which he lived. Rejecting the crudeness and
superstition of his time, Muhammad took a look at the 360
gods of the city of Mecca and believed that the one called
Allah, which simply means "the God," was the one true God.
The only God. A God whose true nature is awesome, fear-
inspiring power.

Muslims believe that one day Muhammad was visited by
an angel who commanded him, "Proclaim!" Muhammad
told the angel that he was not a proclaimer and hurried home,
believing that he was either called to be a prophet or was
turning mad. He began teaching this radical commitment to
one God and developing a teaching about life. After three
years, Muhammad had 40 followers, although most people
were quite hostile to his message. After a decade, however, he
had several hundred followers. In the year 622, Muhammad
fled from Mecca to Medina. There his message was accepted
and he became an administrator, a master politician, a mag-
istrate and a statesman. This is very important in understanding Islam. Muhammad was at once a religious, military and
political leader, and ever since, followers of Islam have held
to a belief system that is both political and religious.

Islam is generally a religion of preaching and proclamation about the right kind of life to live, not of miracles. But
there is one miracle Muslims believe in: the transmission of
the Koran. The Koran is the holy book of Islam. It is four-

fifths the length of the New Testament. Muslims regard the Koran as the literal word of Allah revealed to Muhammad, who wrote down what was given to him over a span of 23 years.

Muslims believe that this revelation is the last and highest revelation of God, following the Old Testament (which centers on the stories of Abraham and Moses), and the gospel of Jesus. Muslims view Jews, Christians and themselves as People of the Book. Unlike the Old Testament and the New Testament, however, the Koran is written as direct speech of God, speaking in the first person. It is seen to be a heavenly word uncorrupted. Non-Muslims find the Koran difficult to read for its density of doctrinal words.

When Medina won the war that broke out between the two kingdoms of Medina and Mecca, Muhammad became the indisputable leader of Arabia, and the beginnings of a new empire were formed. When Muhammad died in 632, Arabia was united under Muhammad's control. By the close of that century, his followers had also conquered Armenia, Persia, Syria, Palestine, Iraq, North Africa and Spain and had crossed the Pyrenees Mountains into France. If the European ruler Charles Martel had not defeated the Muslims in the Battle of Tours in 733, Muslim rule might have extended all the way into Europe. Western history might have been entirely different. The European immigrants who came to America from Poland and German and Norway might not have been Lutherans and Catholics, but Muslims.

Many religions have gotten entangled with militarism and conquest—including Christianity, especially in the Middle Ages. But one historical reality about Islam is that political rule and conquest were part of its inception. Many believe that is one reason why extreme Muslim interpretations even today place an unambiguous label of "infidel" on Christians, Jews and Westerners and why non-Muslims living in Muslim-dominated lands are considered *dhimmi,* a definite second-class citizenship.

The posture of Islam toward the rest of the world began with Muhammad. For the Muslim, there is unbounded respect and admiration for Muhammad. He was a shepherd, a hermit, a soldier, a politician and the writer of mystical writings. Yet the Muslim is insulted by the old-fashioned word "Mohammedanism." They maintain that Allah is the focus of their faith, and Muhammad is only a prophet. In contrast, in Christianity, Jesus Himself is the object of faith. It is *Christ*ianity, not *Peter*ianity or *Paul*ianity. Today it is believed that more boys are named Muhammad than any other name in the world.[2]

"Islam" means "submission," and "Muslim" means "one who has submitted his life to God." Islam focuses on the total submission of one's life to a lifestyle based on law. Islam is more a religion of deed than belief. It is appealing to some because it is so concrete and specific in what it requires. Sexual immorality is prohibited, as are intoxicates and gambling. The main requirements, however, are delineated in what are known as the Five Pillars of Islam.

The first pillar is the profession of belief required of all Muslims, the *shahadah.* This creed of Islam is extremely simple: "There is no god but Allah, and Muhammad is his prophet." All it takes to become a Muslim is to publicly recite that phrase with sincerity of heart. The second pillar is prayer five times a day. (You're probably familiar with the scene of dozens, hundreds or thousands of people kneeling together in prayer—a powerful and binding ritual for Muslims.) The third pillar is charity. Giving 2 percent of your profit to help those who are less fortunate is a fundamental act of mercy. The fourth pillar is observing the holy month of Ramadan, which includes fasting from food and drink from sunup to sundown. And the fifth pillar is the requirement of a pilgrimage to Mecca once in the Muslim's lifetime.

Part of the appeal of Islam is how straightforward it is. No matter what country you come from, whether you are Arab or Indonesian or African-American, to become a Muslim, you begin by reciting the simple creed: "There is no god but Allah, and Muhammad is his prophet" and agree to a set of specific, concrete rules. It is a form of religion that many seek.

One day Jesus was asked, "What must we do to do the works God requires?" (John 6:28). It's likely that each person in the crowd was hoping to get a short list of rules, perhaps something akin to the five pillars. "Lay it on the line, Jesus, and I'll hop right to it. God wants it; He'll get it. He'll be pleased, and I'll be justified." But Jesus looked at the people and said, "The work of God is this: to believe in the one he has sent" (John 6:29). Amazing. Unexpected. Simple, but powerful. According to Jesus, God is looking for something much more than a lifestyle based on law. He is looking for a faith relationship out of which come not merely conformity of behavior, but spiritual character and connection with divine power. This is how a human life tainted by sin is cleansed and reshaped. Life ethics are shaped by the power of faith relationship.

Over the centuries, Islam spread well beyond Arabia. Much of that 1,400 years has been a history of war. A conviction that has been called a "sixth pillar" of Islam is *jihad,* which means "exertion or struggle." Sometimes Muslims have thought of *jihad* as the struggle for true religion in a chaotic world, and sometimes *jihad* has meant a holy war—the taking up of arms in a just cause.

For obvious reasons, people today want to understand the global conflict between Muslims and non-Muslims. We look at the World Trade Center tragedy and other terrorist acts and we ask ourselves, *How can these things possibly be?* We know that these were not the attacks of *all* Muslims, but they were the acts of *some* Muslims.

Samuel P. Huntington is a professor at Harvard University and the author of a fascinating book called *The Clash of Civilizations and the Remaking of World Order,* written before September 11. Huntington says that the causes of contemporary Muslim wars lie in politics, not seventh-century religious doctrines. He gives several reasons for the rise of radical Islam in the modern world:

- There's a resurgence of Islamic consciousness, movements and identity, a response to modernization and globalization and secularization.

- Throughout the Muslim world, there is a sense of grievance, resentment and hostility toward the West and its wealth, power and culture, prompted by Western domination of the Muslim world for much of the twentieth century.

- There are bitter divisions within the Muslim world (tribal, religious, ethnic, political and cultural) and there is no single dominating Muslim state today.

- High birthrates in Muslim countries have produced an explosion of youths, particularly males between 16 and 30 years old who may be educated or uneducated but are unemployed. They are the ones joining radical organizations like guerilla groups and terrorist networks. Young males are the principal perpetrators of violence in all societies, and they exist in abundant numbers in Muslim societies.[3]

Could all of this become a war between civilizations, not just one country against another country or even one ideology against another ideology—whole civilizations set against each other? This is the desired goal of people like Osama bin Laden, although one of the things preventing such a development today is that Islam is not united. There are many different factions. The sobering fact is that radical Islam includes not just a few thousand terrorists, but tens of millions of Muslims. *Newsweek* reported:

If we recognize that the underlying struggle is not just with actual terrorists but with radical Islamists who see the world as a Manichaean struggle of believers and nonbelievers, then we are not talking about a small and isolated group of fanatics. Osama bin Laden has evoked substantial sympathy throughout the Muslim world since September 11 for standing up to the United States, from slum dwellers in Karachi to professionals in Beirut and Cairo, to Pakistani and Algerian citizens in Britain and France. The Middle East specialist Daniel Pipes estimates this radicalized population to be some 10 to 15 percent of the Muslim world.[4]

So what do we learn when we compare Islam, which has some interest in Jesus, with the historic Christian view of Jesus? In Christianity, of central importance is the fact that Jesus Christ *is* the speech of God. The New Testament book of Hebrews begins with this statement:

> In the past God spoke to our forefathers through the prophets at many times and in various ways, but in these last days he has spoken to us by his Son, whom he appointed heir of all things, and through whom he made the universe (1:1-2).

In Islam, the Koran is centrally important, because it is believed to be the recitation of God. The Bible, on the other hand, describes Jesus *as* the speech of God, the Word of God. Many people have observed, in fact, that Jesus is to Christianity what the Koran is to Islam. The difference, of course, is that Jesus is a living Word of God—God Himself—speaking to humanity with a clarity and brilliance and depth and character and beauty that is unlike what any other religious theory in the world has conceived.

Christians believe that God has been speaking throughout human history. Abraham, Moses, Isaiah, Jeremiah and many others delivered diverse messages of God. God spoke through the poetry of the psalms and the oracles of the prophets, on Mount Sinai and even in historical events themselves. But in these last days, something different has happened. The Son of God has spoken—and so God has spoken. God's speech through the prophets is an amazing thing. The fact that He spoke at many times and in many different ways is all the more amazing. But when the very Son of God came, God's revelation became personal and direct.

In Islam, Jesus is held in high regard. He is seen as a prophet, as born of a virgin and as the Messiah, but not as the Son of God, not God incarnate. The Koran teaches that "it is not worthy of God that He should take a son" (19:92). It would drag God down to speak of Him as the father of anybody—of Jesus *or* of us. Muhammad was exposed to Christians in Arabia early in his life, but he said some really strange things about their beliefs. For example, the idea that Christians worship a Trinity consisting of the Father, the Virgin Mary (to whom the Father was married) and the Son, Jesus (5:116). This is a convoluted representation of Christianity that Muhammad rejected. It's possible that he met some people who considered themselves Christians who had terribly warped beliefs.

In contrast to the Koran, the New Testament portrays Jesus as the Son of God in a unique sense and says that we are invited by God to be His children by faith, to view Him as a loving and powerful Father and to address Him as such.

Hebrews 1:3 says that Jesus "is the radiance of God's glory." That means that the very essence of God's being shines through Jesus, because He belongs to that being. As surely as you cannot separate the sun from its rays, we cannot separate God the Father from the Son and the Holy Spirit. Jesus is the "exact representation of [God's] being" (Heb. 1:3). The Greek word used in this phrase means "character" or "stamp," and it suggests the impression made by a die. A stamp leaves in what is stamped an exact duplicate of the stamp itself. That is why Jesus said, "Anyone who has seen me has seen the Father" (John 14:9) and "Believe in God, believe also in me" (John 14:1, *NRSV*). It is the very reason why we can have confidence that we can know God. In the past, God used prophets, but now He has spoken to us in the Person of His Son.

Hebrews 1:3 goes on to say that Jesus "provided purification for sins." Chapter 2 verse 10 tells us that Jesus is the author of our salvation because of His suffering, and chapter 2 verse 14 says that Jesus destroyed the power of death and the devil, and freed "those who . . . were held in slavery by their fear of death." Although Islam regards Jesus as a prophet, it does not view Him as the Savior. He does not atone for sins—you alone must pay for your sins. Furthermore, the Koran says Jesus was not crucified, but somebody was mistakenly crucified in a case of mistaken identity (4:157). And if Jesus didn't die, then there is no resurrection either.

Hebrews 1:8-13 also clearly describes Jesus as the Lord of heaven and Earth. The Lord Jesus was there when the foundations of the earth were laid, He rules over His enemies, and His throne lasts forever and ever.

In Islam, Jesus is a prophet in a long line of ascending prophets, beginning with Adam and going through Abraham, then the great prophet Moses, then the greater Jesus and finally the greatest and final prophet, Muhammad (the "seal of the prophets," according to Koran 33:40). Hence the creed of Islam, which is recited five times a day, every day, by devout Muslims: "There is no god but Allah, and Muhammad is his prophet."

But in the Christian faith, Jesus is the Creator and Lord of a people who are gathered together at the foot of His cross in thanksgiving for forgiveness and cleansing. Jesus knows how far short we have all fallen, yet He loved us enough to give His life for us, paying a price we couldn't pay ourselves. He points to life, not death and conquest.

Because of the empty tomb, His followers believe that their Lord is still on the loose.

Notes

1. Charles Colson, *Tough Questions About God, Faith, and Life* (Carol Stream, IL: Tyndale House Publishers, 2006), p. 208.
2. Nick Wyck, "Muhammad—The Most Popular Name in the World?" TimesOnline, January 23, 2007. http://women.timesonline.co.uk/tol/life_and_style/women/families/book_of_names/article1183264.ece (accessed June 2007).
3. Samuel P. Huntington, *The Clash of Civilizations* (New York: Simon and Schuster, 1996), pp. 263-265.
4. Francis Fukuyama, "Their Target: The Modern World," *Newsweek*, December 17, 2001, p. 42.

CHAPTER 12

Credo: I Believe This About God

I was sitting in the ballroom of one of the nicest hotels in town for the annual prayer breakfast sponsored by our state's governor. I and seven others at the round table at which we sat were finishing the typical scrambled-egg-and-orange-juice breakfast, just as a hundred other tables were doing the same thing. These prayer breakfasts are interdenominational and interfaith affairs, so the speakers have quite a challenge on their hands. How do you lead in prayer when in the room there are Christians, Jews, Muslims, Hindus and others who have entirely different ideas about prayer and forms of prayer? One of the speakers stepped to the microphone and attempted to solve the dilemma in a unique way. He said that since human language is so far below the mind of God that it will always be like a child's chatter, we should think of our prayers like offering the unformed and primitive letters of the alphabet—and God has to make sense of our prayers. And then he paused.

And with that, he invited the hundreds of people gathered to join him in a prayer that would be simply the recitation of the alphabet.

"So then, let us pray. A-B-C-D . . ." Slowly. Painfully. I was stunned, as were most of the people in the room. *He is actually doing this.* I could tell others were stunned too, even though they went along with it.

For the first third of the alphabet, I was thinking, *I can't believe we're doing this;* and the other thing I was thinking was, *Don't look up at your friends at the table—you don't want to see the incredulous look in their eyes and risk an uncontrollable laugh.* For the middle third of the alphabet the crowd mindlessly droned on. And the last third was a kind of sprint to the finish, despite the pacing of the speaker, and a huge sense of relief when we got to ". . . X-Y-Z-Amen!"

Now I have to give the fellow credit for creativity, and I'm sure he meant well, but I believe his plan backfired. Prayer is human language at the highest level, even when it is the voice of children talking to a heavenly Father.

In previous chapters, we summarized some of the essential tenets of Buddhism, Hinduism, Islam and other belief systems. Now we turn to the Christian response to the drive that says, "I want to believe."

In this and the following chapter, we will be looking at some of the specific beliefs of the Christian faith. If we are to talk meaningfully about believing, we have to get to *what* we believe. There is no point in talking generically about "being religious" or "being spiritual." Faith has content. Faith is not an alphabet soup—it is a real language with real meaning.

At a personal level, there are many options open to us when we realize that we have a deep drive to believe. You could let it carry you casually along a window-shopping stroll of faith—always looking, never committing. You could latch onto a few black and white convictions, put your stake in the ground and say, "Okay, now I know where I belong, where I stand, what I believe. Mission accomplished. Search over."

Or you could let the drive to believe keep your eyes open, your mind calculating, your conscience soft, your spirit alert.

The one thing that will be most unsatisfying is to not feed the hunger to believe. To let the longing linger—disengaged, unattached, unfulfilled. Hunger is not just an ache, it is a warning: Better eat, or you'll die.

But it is not enough to say, "I believe." This is just the preface to the stance you've taken for your life. You believe what? You believe in what? You believe in whom? That deepest drive we have—the drive to believe—has a created purpose. It is to carry us to places we would not go if we were just giraffes or alligators or eagles. Human beings are created to seek and to keep seeking until our last breath, when we cross over the line and discover so many things we could have discovered in this life if we hadn't wasted so much time.

We hunger so that we know it's time to eat. We thirst so that we look for water and our bodies don't dry out. We become infatuated so that love can be born, and we marry and have children and carry the human race forward another step.

And we long to believe so that we keep looking for God, keep seeking the truth, keep asking for answers and keep knocking on doors that promise to open into whole new worlds. We know this is right. Jesus told us, "Ask and it will be given to you; seek and you will find; knock and the door will be opened to you" (Luke 11:9). It is the finding, the opening and the receiving that allow us to say, "I believe *this* . . ."

If you were a person living in the great city of Rome about A.D. 150 and had come to be captivated by the message of Jesus, which continued to be passed along generations after His life, you might signal that you wanted to become a part of the Christian congregation in that city—that you wanted to go from attending Christian meetings and listening to teachings to being an actual follower. And if you did that, the leaders of the congregation would invite you into a small class in which you'd be able to learn the essence of the faith so that, if you chose, you could be baptized and confess what you believe: "I believe in God the Father, Almighty, Maker of heaven and Earth, and in Jesus Christ, His only Son, our Lord . . ." This statement, known as the Roman Symbol, may have been read to the person being baptized: "Do you believe in God the Father Almighty, Maker of heaven and Earth?" And if the answer was yes, then on to the next question: "Do you believe in Jesus Christ, His only Son, our Lord?" And so it went, the person going on record, giving voice to the firm convictions of mind and heart, not knowing what would happen to family relationships, not knowing whether the next emperor would try to round up the Christians again, not knowing if the next time he or she might be among those taken.

Later adaptations of the Roman Symbol became known as the Apostles' Creed, and in its first Latin word is summed up our deepest drive: *Credo*, "I believe." Not just "I *want* to believe," but "I *do* believe." Someone has said that, of all the bold things a human being can do, there are few that are bolder than to stand in front of others and to say, "I believe *this*."

Now the Apostles' Creed, which, in English translation, is a few dozen words long, is not an exhaustive statement of Christian belief. It is the essence, the core, as it was perceived by the first generations of Christians. (It was not written by the original apostles, but was assumed to represent their core teaching.) It has stood the test of time. Like all creeds, it serves the function of taking the dynamic of the act of believing—

credo—and making it an objective statement, a creed. Some people think of creeds as limiting and bound by time and place, or as too ecclesiastical. But almost all churches have some kind of "statement of faith." We do this because we know that if faith is only personal experience, we will ride the roller coaster of our own subjectivity. We may move in and out of faith, rather than knowing that "the faith" is bigger than our personal acts of faith. Creeds and statements of faith remind us that what we believe in is bigger than our drive to believe.

There is no one creed that says it all, and most creeds need to be translated across cultural lines and across time. One of the most remarkable things about Christian faith is how many different cultures it has taken root in. Like a plant that can grow in any kind of soil or climate, in places with wildly different amounts of light and darkness, Christian faith has been the liberating truth of people living in animistic tribes and in the oak hallways of centuries-old universities—and everyone in between.

The Masai people of Eastern Africa are tall, lean and mysterious. They are mighty warriors. Their metal jewelry gleams against their dark-brown skin. They live in small huts in the countryside. While many African tribes have lost much of their culture, the Masai have continued to practice their ancient rituals and ceremonies and have maintained their social order and warrior ways. They are a long way from Rome in A.D. 150. About 50 years ago some missionaries paraphrased the Apostles' Creed in a way that would communicate the faith to the Masai:

> We believe in the one High God, who out of love created the beautiful world and everything good in it. He created man and wanted man to be happy in

the world. God loves the world and every nation and tribe on the earth. We have known this High God in darkness, and now we know him in the light. God promised in the book of his word, the Bible, that he would save the world and all the nations and tribes.

We believe that God made good his promise by sending his son, Jesus Christ, a man in the flesh, a Jew by tribe, born poor in a little village, who left his home and was always on safari doing good, curing people by the power of God, teaching about God and man, showing the meaning of religion is love. He was rejected by his people, tortured and nailed hands and feet to a cross, and died. He lay buried in the grave, but the hyenas did not touch him, and on the third day, he rose from the grave. He ascended to the skies. He is the Lord.

We believe that all our sins are forgiven through him. All who have faith in him must be sorry for their sins, be baptized in the Holy Spirit of God, live the rules of love and share the bread together in love, to announce the good news to others until Jesus comes again. We are waiting for him. He is alive. He lives. This we believe. Amen.[1]

Maybe as you read that you thought, *I'm not Masai, but that will do for me.* Maybe you analyzed it word by word, focusing on the phrases you wouldn't agree with. (That's what we often do with statements of faith—zero in on what we don't like, what we'd like to start an argument about, rather than be carried along by at least some of the powerful content.)

"We believe all our sins are forgiven through him." That's plain and forceful. It's a proclamation—a belief you want to shout, not whisper. "God loves the world and every nation and tribe on the earth." That is something you want to know if you belong to a minority group that some people would deem primitive and less than fully human. Love comes up numerous times in this statement: God's love, the necessity for love, living by "the rules of love." This creed connects the three things the Bible says will never fail: faith, hope and love.

Jesus' dwelling among us becomes "he was always on safari." The fact that His body did not suffer decay becomes "the hyenas did not touch him." The return of Christ becomes "we are waiting for him," a statement that He will in fact return but goes further and makes an application for us: We're waiting. Believing means living your life with the excitement of knowing that any day the King could walk through your door. That changes your life.

Let's come back to the Apostles' Creed, because it is a historic marker, the template on which most Christian confessions of faith have been based. Here is the whole statement:

> *I believe in God the Father Almighty,*
> *Maker of heaven and earth.*
> *And in Jesus Christ his only Son our Lord,*
> *who was conceived by the Holy Ghost,*
> *born of the Virgin Mary, suffered under Pontius Pilate,*
> *was crucified, dead, and buried; he descended into hell;*
> *the third day he rose again from the dead;*
> *he ascended into heaven,*
> *and sitteth on the right hand of God the Father Almighty;*
> *from thence he shall come to judge the quick and the dead.*

I believe in the Holy Ghost; the holy catholic Church,
the communion of saints,
the forgiveness of sins, the resurrection of the body,
and the life everlasting.
Amen.

I believe in God. The spotlight is on us when we say, "I believe," but the focus suddenly spins in the opposite direction when these words are added: "in God." Believing is something that happens in us, but the kind of believing that is good and reliable is not about us at all. Believing is about what is out there, about *who* is out there.

I have never visited the sunken city of Atlantis or the bustling city of Hong Kong. I could believe in Atlantis, if someone showed me it was more than a legend; but I can actually go to Hong Kong (although, because I've never been to Hong Kong, I have to take it by faith that it is actually out there). So I believe there is a Hong Kong because there is very good evidence for it. But my belief does not make the place real. The hustle and bustle and vivacity of Hong Kong goes on whether I believe in it or not. And I would never say, "Well, believing in the existence of Hong Kong is okay for you, but for me, I just don't believe it, and that's okay."

So the person who believes in God is, as a very first step, taking a step of humility (always a healthy and sensible thing to do). The person is actually saying, "I have come to know that I am not the center of the universe. I am not the supreme being of my life. I am not the strongest force shaping my life."

I believe in God *the Father.* This is a short way of saying, "I know that there is, among the powerful, beautiful, right things of life, a Most Powerful, Most Beautiful, Most Just, Most Gracious Being. I believe that He is personal, which is the point of 'God *the Father.*' I know He protects us—not by taking us out of this pain-filled world, but by being with us in this world. I know He provides for us—nobody else causes grain to grow up out of soil or keeps our hearts in rhythm. I know He guides us like a good Father, speaking to us with every passing year about what is right and wrong."

Some people worry that the creeds and the Bible itself are limiting because God is referred to as male. Does this leave half the human race out of the equation? Removed from God and unable to have a direct relationship with Him? To put it crassly: Is God the leader of a boys-only club, and this is why women have suffered discrimination and abuse? No, there can't possibly be gender discrimination in God Himself. It is true that the Bible refers to God as Father, intending that we take from that all the positive connotations of a personal protector and provider. God is also referred to as a nurturer in many passages of Scripture, Jesus Himself saying that He wished He could gather His people, like a hen gathers her chicks (see Matt. 23:37; Luke 13:34, to use just one example). Furthermore, Genesis 1:27 says that God made man in His image, male and female. The image of God is equally present in both men and women. After all, where do all created characteristics come from if not from the Creator? God is not a man or a woman. And God is not really male or female either. God is above all such distinctions. We don't spend any time wondering whether God is European or Asian or African. He is above all this. But so that we can know God truly and be comforted and guided by His goodness, He is "the Father."

I believe God the Father is *Almighty*. He is mighty in every way, at all times and under all circumstances. Young people may grow weary, but the Lord God's strength never fades, so we can rise up on the wings of eagles (see Isa. 40:31).

I believe God is *Maker of heaven and earth*. This is in reference to the opening statement of the Bible, Genesis 1:1: "In the beginning God created the heavens and the earth." This answers the largest of questions all people have: How did we get here? How did all this get here? Is there a purpose to all this?

The answer? God willed light into existence. "Let there be light" (v. 3) and there was. He formed both atom and universe. He made something out of nothing; He made everything out of nothing. And then He really got to work, creating things that swim and things that fly and things that crawl and dig and walk and run. Things that make you smile, things that make your jaw drop, things that make you run away. Tigers and toads, hawks and hyenas, squirrels and pearls and girls. Not just one kind of tree, but hundreds of species. Not just things that live in the light, but things that swim deeper and darker than any of us have ever seen. Why create something that human beings never get to see? Because He wanted to. There was no necessity whereby God had to create. That is the reason we have to believe life is a continual adventure. God did not create the universe to impress us. God's mission is not to entertain the human race. That's one of the ways we know that believing is not about us. We get to experience wonder, not merely enjoyment.

The creation is an exuberant explosion of the magnificence of God, and none of us ever knows what we are going to discover next. This also gives our lives nobility. Because God did not *have* to create us but *chose* to, every day of our lives we can say with certainty, "I am here because the Almighty Creator *wanted* me to be here. So go ahead, criticize me, demean me, discard me; but that will not change the truth that I am here because God wanted me." God's power in creation is further shown in the desire He has put in us to create.

And then there is heaven. He is *Maker of heaven* and Earth. We probe the heavens with telescopes and spectrometers and other instruments of astronomy, and every time the Hubble telescope discovers a new formation deep in the galaxy, it produces awe.

But "heaven" also means the invisible. The realm of God that no human eye has yet to see. Is this too much of a stretch? Modern physics tells us we must accept the existence of particles we will never see, because well-grounded theory tells us they must exist. So is it too much to believe that there is an invisible spiritual realm beyond our five senses?

Why did God create all this? Because He wanted to. He chose to. He enjoyed doing it. God is the one behind everything, above everything, beneath everything. We don't believe in God because we've finally tracked Him down and found Him in a remote part of the world hiding in a cave. We believe in God when we open our eyes and see Him all around. When we realize that we are the ones hiding in the shadows. We are the ones who need to be found. We were not lost because God could not find us. We became lost when we did anything that disconnected us from our Father.

No wonder we want to believe.

Now if you say you believe in God the Father Almighty, Maker of heaven and Earth, you have already established a substantial base of faith—and you've excluded other beliefs.

You've excluded polytheism: If there is one and only one God, then there cannot be multiple gods. You've excluded pantheism: A Creator God who is personal cannot be at the same time an impersonal energy that pervades all things. You've excluded Gnosticism (either in its ancient form or in its recent resurgence): The Gnostics believed the created realm was a mistake.

To put it more positively, by saying "I believe *this*," you have begun a journey in which this personal, almighty God is going to take you to places you never could have imagined, and He'll explain all the parts of life that have seemed mixed up and mysterious.

And that brings us to the second major confession of the Creed: I believe *in Jesus Christ his only Son our Lord, who was conceived by the Holy Ghost, born of the Virgin Mary, suffered under Pontius Pilate, was crucified, dead, and buried; he descended into hell; the third day he rose again from the dead; he ascended into heaven, and sitteth on the right hand of God the Father Almighty; from thence he shall come to judge the quick and the dead.*

There is a lot of detail here. Some people believe all of it, others some of it, and still others none of it. When you look at the Apostle's Creed, you notice that some very important beliefs are mentioned with just a phrase: "the Holy Ghost," "the forgiveness of sins" and "life everlasting." But the statement about Jesus is expansive. There are two reasons for this:

1. *Jesus is the great mystery.* When the Bible uses "mystery," it doesn't mean a riddle—it means something that is so much higher and greater than who we are that our feeble minds stretch to comprehend even part of it.

2. *Jesus is the great controversy.* He said He came to
   seek and to save the lost. To stand before people
   who say, "I want to believe," and say, "Believe *in
   Me.*" Someone showed up 2,000 years ago and
   said, "I am the Son of God."

Jesus said it. The Father said it about Jesus at His baptism and transfiguration: A voice from heaven said, "This
is my Son, whom I love" (Matt. 3:17) and "This is my Son . . .
Listen to him!" (Mark 9:7). And the perspective of the
Gospels and the rest of the New Testament is not that Jesus
was Son of God in terms of being created by God or the
offspring of God like we are. Jesus' antagonists picked up
stones to kill Him because they recognized that the way in
which He was using "Son of God" and "Son of Man"
amounted to a claim that He was the unique One who
would come, the One who would save.

I believe in Jesus Christ His only Son *our Lord.* In Acts 10,
Peter, the Jewish fisherman and leader of a new revolutionary movement, found himself—shockingly, amazingly—in
the home of a Gentile named Cornelius. Prompted by God
to say "I believe this" to people he considered beyond the
possibility of belief, he found himself explaining how the
Jewish Messiah was for the world:

> I now realize how true it is that God does not show
> favoritism but accepts people from every nation who
> fear him and do what is right. You know the message
> God sent to the people of Israel, telling the good
> news of peace through Jesus Christ, who is Lord of
> all (Acts 10:34-36).

Peter probably couldn't believe those words were coming out of his own mouth. "Lord of all." It was enough of a stretch to believe He was the long-awaited Messiah for the people of Israel, but to believe that He was sent for the world? This thing, this faith, was getting larger and larger. Peter must have felt like God was taking his vision to wider and wider perspectives. But how could it be any other way? If Jesus was the divine Son sent to save, how could that not be for any and all? If He was Lord of some, how could He not be Lord of all? Lordship, in the divine sense, is not control over a select, exclusive, elite set of people. He is Lord of all.

Conceived by the Holy Ghost. If the prior statements are true—that Jesus Christ is the Son of God and our Lord— then it is not surprising that He would come to the world in a demonstration of divine power. Jesus' mother, Mary, said to the angel, "But I'm a virgin. How will I bear a child?" (see Luke 1:34). And the angel answered, "The Holy Spirit will come upon you, and the power of the Most High will overshadow you. So the holy one to be born will be called the Son of God" (Luke 1:35).

Jesus was not born of a virgin because God needed a way to enter the human race and wanted to avoid the normal way babies are born. The virgin birth of Jesus was simply and purely the leading miracle of a life of miracles. It was God saying, as He always does with miracles, "Let Me show you something that is so out of the ordinary, you have to know that I have done it." It was the Son of God entering the stage of humanity with the curtain drawn back and with a chorus of angels and the spotlight of the star of Bethlehem.

I don't have a hard time at all believing that Jesus was born of a virgin. I am just as amazed that God could take the tiniest of seeds from my wife and myself, join them together and bring to life that son and daughter who are now quickly approaching adulthood. I'll never get over that. The virginal conception of Jesus is only too hard to believe if one assumes that nothing in the world ever happens just once. But why would we ever think God is limited to what is normal (which He determines anyway)?

I believe He *suffered . . . was crucified, dead, and buried; he . . . shall come to judge the quick and the dead.* This belief reflects the clear history told in the Gospels and explained in the rest of the New Testament. But it needed to be said in the Apostle's Creed because, as the early Christians were figuring out their faith, there were some who believed a divine Savior made sense, but (like a lot of the esoteric religions of the day held) such a savior figure could not have been human. So the epistle of 1 John 4 says that true believers believe Jesus came "in the flesh" (v. 2). And of the dozens of statements in the New Testament that describe the meaning and effects of the real suffering and real death of Jesus, Ephesians 2:13-14 puts it well: "But now in Christ Jesus you who once were far away have been brought near through the blood of Christ. For he himself is our peace."

The death of Jesus was not the end of the story.

I recently saw the film *United 93,* which tells the story of that airplane and its passengers on September 11, 2001. Sixty-three passengers, highjacked. Men and women, young and old, hearing on cell phones what has happened within the past hour at the World Trade Center. A desperate and courageous plan to rush the highjackers and wrest control of the plane from them. A struggle that lasted 10 minutes but seemed like an eternity. They tear off the cockpit door, are near to saving themselves, the plane goes nose down. And then, the screen goes black, silence. Soon, words of tribute are on the screen.

I wasn't expecting to be so deeply moved by this film. I already knew the story—or so I thought. I wondered whether the last moments might be difficult in their finality. But what I wasn't expecting was to be drawn into the gradually unfolding crisis, from the point of view of the people on United 93, of the air traffic controllers and of those at the Air Force headquarters. The plotters were hidden, like a nest of snakes that was about to scatter and strike. But the big impact on me was the transformation of ordinary people into heroes. They fidgeted, they sweated, they prayed, and at the decisive moment, they acted. The end of the story is the death of heroes. Many other stories end with the death of the hero. And even if the screen goes black, you know that the nobility of the heroes goes on.

In Jesus Christ, however, the screen (figuratively speaking) goes black for a moment. There is the blackness of the grave, the darkness of the descent into hades (which, depending on how you translate "descended into hell" either means a descent into the grave or a journey to an invisible realm where He proclaimed the liberation of those people of faith who needed a Savior just like us).

But then the screen is lit up with the brilliant light of the resurrection.

Now there are those who believe that Jesus was a hero figure like others who gave their lives for what they stood for. That He tried His hardest to pull the plane out of its spiral into the ground. That He made a difference because of how valiantly He stood for truth.

But for 2,000 years, most who consider Jesus the Savior take in the whole account of His life, which began in Bethlehem, paused on the brow of a hill outside Jerusalem and then burst out of a broken tomb. I believe this. He suffered, He was crucified, He really died, He was buried, He descended—but then He rose from death; later He ascended into the skies in the clear sight of witnesses, and now, at the right hand of God the Father, He reigns supreme and will come again, at which time all accounts will be settled. Every wrong will be condemned. Every right thing vindicated. Or the way Jesus Himself put it: The Son of Man will come in glory, the nations gathered before Him, and He will say to those on His right, "Come . . . take your inheritance, the kingdom prepared for you since the creation of the world" (Matt. 25:34).

Multitudes of people believe who want to believe it. Not because it is wishful thinking. Not because it is the easiest thing to believe. The easiest thing is to think that we will all take the rank in eternity that matches how hard we worked on Earth. Maybe a few of us will even be heroes.

But that's to believe not much more than that maybe someone will remember you as a well-intentioned person whose life ended with a blank screen.

Now there is one more statement in the Creed that has to do with God, before it moves on to issues of life: *I believe in the Holy Ghost.*

"Ghost" is a very old English expression that meant "spirit" 400 years ago when the *King James Version* of the Bible was translated, but that today has all kinds of connotations of hauntings and roamings—none of which has anything to do with the nature of God, of course. So in virtually all modern renderings of the Creed, "I believe in the Holy Ghost" is "I believe in the Holy Spirit" (as is also reflected in all modern translations of the Bible).

There are no details here about the Holy Spirit—unlike the Son, Jesus—because there were few controversies about the Holy Spirit in the early decades of Christianity.

In Scripture, God is described as "spirit," which is a way of saying that God is not a material being. God is invisible, but real and powerful nonetheless (like the wind, which comes from unseen directions but is immensely powerful nonetheless, as Jesus said in John 3). In the New Testament, the Holy Spirit is divine but distinguishable from God the Father and from Jesus, the Son of God. The Holy Spirit guides and empowers believers. It is possible for a mortal human being to live in the Spirit (see Rom. 8:4-5) and to walk by the Spirit (see Gal. 5:25), and because this living and walking is an intimate and personal relationship with God, one can "grieve the Holy Spirit" (Eph. 4:30) or quench the Holy Spirit (see 1 Thess. 5:19).

From beginning to end in Christian thought, God is personal. A Father for the fatherless. The Son: Jesus Christ, who is Master, Friend and the Shepherd who gave up His life for His sheep. And the Holy Spirit: mysterious in many ways, invisible to the eye, but a personal divine presence who lives and works in the inner sanctum of the believer's spiritual life, giving understanding, wisdom, power, guidance, and much more.

As we mentioned at the start of this book, our tendency when talking about faith and belief is to focus on ourselves—

our experience of finding and living in faith. But the majority of the Apostles Creed—which says, "This is what I believe about God—Father, Christ, Spirit"—is a whole different emphasis on God as the object, not us as the subjects, of belief. For early Christian believers, it made perfect sense to talk about, worship and pray to God the Father, the Son and the Spirit, while all the time believing, in the Hebrew tradition, that there is only one God. A later generation of Christians wrapped words around this belief. They called God a *trinitas* in Latin, "Trinity" in English: something (or rather, Someone) who is able to be one and three at the same time. Naturally this became a point of debate between Christians and non-Christians (and, in the finer details, a debate between Christians). But the consensus of historic Christianity is that we should not be surprised when the character and reality of God turn out to be mysterious and beyond our normal rules of arithmetic and other empirical constraints.

This is not a cop-out, not a desperate attempt to strain the dictates of logic. For Christians, the Trinity is an overwhelming statement of the power of the personal God who invites us to be transformed by worshiping and relating to Father, Christ and Spirit, who are themselves (mysteriously) in relationship to one another.

And then there are all kinds of things we can believe about life, which we come to next.

Note
1. Vincent J. Donovan, *Christianity Rediscovered* (Maryknoll, NY: Orbis Books, 2003), p. 148.

CHAPTER 13

Credo: I Believe This About Life

It was gloomy and cold in Cluj, Romania, the day I visited the church of my friend Mircea, who has been a pastor there for 15 years. But inside the church, all those gathered, already singing, were filling the room with lightness and joy. All the generations were there: young boys and girls sitting together in their own section, some of them readying themselves to sing one of the songs for the morning; the middle-aged; and the older men and women whose faces showed a lot of the wear of their years. For anyone 20 years or older, the history of living under the oppression of Communism is a fixed memory—and you can read it in their eyes.

Mircea grew up in a home where believing was discouraged. His father was a radically committed Communist, and that meant absolute allegiance to the state and its ideal of the classless society and the philosophy of materialism. For Mircea's father and others like him, God was a myth of the past, and history was moving toward an ideal equilibrium of the classes. They believed that the state had the right and authority and power to move citizens into the mold that would carry out this ideal. But there was very little ideal about it. No utopia emerged from the struggle of the classes—

only more struggle. Power was not used to empower the people but to expand the power of the powerful.

For Mircea, even decades of living in a comprehensive ideology could not suppress the desire to believe. He became a believer in Jesus when he was a young man. He was an embarrassment to his father. He was active in the Christian underground, distributing literature and arranging classes for pastors and other leaders, who would meet in remote rural locations. Then one day the Securitate, the feared Romanian secret police, showed up—three men in a car, Mircea snatched away. They tried to recruit him to be an informant so that they could catch the leaders of the underground church, not knowing that Mircea himself was one of the leaders and one of the most active and effective distributors of Christian literature.

He refused to cooperate. They bound his hands behind his back and made him lie on the floor on his stomach. They beat him mercilessly with a hard rubber truncheon on the bottoms of his feet, but even with pain shooting through his body and his breathing labored, Mircea refused to acquiesce. Four times that dreary November night the interrogators returned. At midnight they released him. For the next three hours Mircea crawled through the city on his hands and knees to get home.

The following day, Mircea was arrested again. The officer in charge kicked him in the back, which sent him slamming into a wall, and said, "Go, you garbage! In less than three months you will be no more. Your wife will go to another man and your children will be on the streets. Then you will know that in this country there is no God but the secret police!"

When Mircea tells you his story, this is when he gets most emphatic. "But the Securitate did not know that in just half that time, six weeks from then, in the latter half of December 1989, the revolution would happen, Communism would fall, and *they* would be no more."

Another Romanian friend, Lucian, told me about that December—about how in Timisoara the revolution began when tens of thousands of people gathered in the town square. And it all began in a most unexpected way: A pastor of a church was being moved to a different city—manipulated by the authorities against his will. A small protest developed outside the church in the city square, and it grew. Between December 18 and 22, 1989, the crowd grew every day. Hundreds, then thousands, then tens of thousands. They chanted, "God is alive. God is alive." This singular belief, which the Communist regime had tried to expunge from the minds of the people over decades of ideological domination—this belief that God is real—had not been extinguished. Lucian was there in the square. His friend Mitica was there. They watched as the authorities occasionally shot some of the protesters—350 died before it was all over. But the crowds were not deterred. Word came to President Ceausescu of the uprising in Timisoara and he rushed back to Romania. Ceausescu and his regime considered bombing the city. They assumed the uprising would be contained in the one city. But news of the protests spread, and soon other major cities rose up. When the president tried to control a crowd in Bucharest and failed, he fled in his personal helicopter, only to be arrested by the army, put on trial and summarily executed by firing squad. It was December 24, Christmas Eve. The Christmas of 1989 in Romania was a new birth for a country.

Mircea, Lucian and Mitica are now all pastors of thriving churches in Romania. And new churches spring up in the country every week.

I've asked myself for years, *What would I say if I stood before a man with a weapon in his hand and he demanded that I recant what I believe?* I hope I would have the kind of faith Mircea had and has, because I know that's real faith.

A faith that is merely a casual flirtation with believing will never stand that kind of test. But if someone can say, "I believe *this*," then he or she may be carried along by the higher power of God. The early Roman Symbol, the core of what became the Apostles' Creed, is a way of going beyond saying "I want to believe" or just "I believe." What is actually being said is "I believe *this*: I believe in God—Father Almighty, Maker of all. I believe in Jesus Christ—Son of God, Lord of all, uniquely born, truly subject to suffering and crucifixion but then risen, ascended and ready to come again when all things will be judged."

And then you come to *I believe in the holy catholic Church*. This is the first of five concluding phrases in the creed, the others being "the communion of the saints, the forgiveness of sins, the resurrection of the body, and the life everlasting." Taken together, these statements are an explosive proclamation of life. It is a way of saying, "Because God is real, I can believe that He is creating a new community, relieving us of the burden of sin and guilt, and giving us hope for the future."

Now it may seem like one thing to say, "I believe in God," but another to say, "I believe in the holy catholic Church." (And, by the way, when the word "catholic" was used in the early Christian era, it meant "universal"—it was not a reference to one Christian tradition versus others, as in "Roman

Catholic Church.") Even if you simplified this confession, taking away the adjectives and just leaving "in the Church," some people would hesitate. *Believing in Jesus is one thing, but dare I believe in the Church?*

The Church is an association of people, and many can only think of all the disappointments they have experienced when they think about it. They hear about molestation charges against priests, the Baptist pastor in their hometown who ran away with the secretary, and the weirdo group that is having members store dry goods and ammunition in their basements that will get them through a seven-year tribulation (the gun and ammunition so that they can blow away anybody who tries to steal their food). Or someone's coolness toward the Church may be because of the oddly anachronistic way really churchy people seem to talk about everything—using a kind of code language, or using words that make it seem as if they somehow missed a couple of centuries of modern advancement.

Then, of course, there is the standard objection: The Church is full of hypocrites. They say they believe one thing, but they do something else.

I find that I have two reactions to this. On the one hand, I sympathize with those who have a disgust for hypocrisy. I'm disgusted with myself when I say one thing but do another. I am mortified when I realize I'm telling my kids that they have to keep their anger under control, and I turn around and fly off the handle at them. I can't help but note that the one group of people that Jesus was bitingly confrontational with was the hypocrites. He called them "whitewashed tombs" (Matt. 23:27)—nice and pretty on the outside but reeking with decay on the inside.

One the other hand, I feel that those who say they won't believe because of the hypocrisy of people in the Church are putting up a smoke screen. We all are very capable of being hypocritical—but what does that have to do with belief in God or even belief in the ideal of the Church? To say "I believe in honesty" while you still have a hard time being honest all the time does not undermine the belief in honesty. It just means that pretty much anyone who is a believer is *in the process* of moving into the reality of what he or she believes. And yes, the Church is full of people just like that. We are all hypocrites at one time or another. But God is not to blame for that. The difficulty we all have with practicing what we believe is exactly why we need God.

That is why we believe and why we want to believe. We want a horizon out there that we can look at and move toward, even if our lives are a long way from the destination.

So to say "I believe in the Church" is not to say "I have found a church that is full of nearly perfect people and I've decided to join it" (which is either a gamble that you will ruin such a great thing or a brash belief that you can improve the gene pool—neither of which seems very logical). To say "I believe in the Church" is a way of saying, "I know that of all the communities I belong to—my hometown, my Rotary Club, my neighborhood association—none of them point me to a higher, eternal purpose. I believe God has something better in mind, that He wants there to be one community that has a divine purpose, can be fulfilling in our lives and can carry out a mission that really saves some people. I believe in the Church."

This is the way the apostle Paul puts it in 2 Corinthians 6:16-18: "We are the temple of the living God. As God has said, 'I will live with them and walk among them, and I will be their God, and they will be my people.' 'Therefore come out from them and be separate, says the Lord. . . . I will be a Father to you, and you will be my sons and daughters.'" If this is true, saying "I believe in the Church" flows directly from "I believe in God the Father Almighty." To believe in God, really believe in God, is to know that you are bound with other people with the same belief, that you relish the life of being a son or daughter of God, of being the people of God, of being a temple, of being the Church. Christians cannot live apart from each other any more than your arms and legs can live and work separately from your torso.

I would most definitely not believe in the Church if I thought it was only a human invention or a sociological trend. But the New Testament turns that completely upside down. It says that God invented the Church (see Matt. 16:18). It is God's way of saying, "I will work in your lives because that is the kind of God I am; but then I will pull you together with others, and because you are all looking to Me as your Father, you are therefore brothers and sisters."

This is what is meant by "holy" Church. Something or someone is holy when set apart by God for a special purpose. A church is holy well before its members start acting holy.

But what is meant by "catholic Church," and why is it that multitudes of churches and most denominations that are not part of the Roman Catholic Church would repeat it again and again? As was mentioned earlier, the adjective "catholic," a translation of the Greek word *katholicos*, means "universal." The phrase was used all over the Christian world in the second century—in Rome, in Alexandria, in Antioch, in Carthage—not as a reference to the church in the city of

Rome (which later became the center of Roman Catholicism), but with its original meaning. The early generations of Christians recognized one thing early on: In contrast to almost all of the religions of the day that were considered to be the special expression of different tribes or countries, Christianity, with its core conviction that God's Son came into the world to be the One who would save everyone living everywhere and was the one Lord of all, was offering a universal solution to a universal spiritual and moral problem in the human race. And it became apparent early on that belief in Jesus Christ moved out very readily across barriers of language and culture and national identity. While the apostles were still alive, Christian faith spread from the Hebrew world to the Greek world to the Latin world. Poor people were coming into the Church, and even members of Caesar's household were believing in Jesus. Men and women. Slaves and slave masters. Nobody had seen anything like this before—a faith that was truly addressing the core issues of humanity so effectively that it had universal appeal.

So the early Christians said that in the same way Jesus is Savior for all and Lord of all, the community of people gathered to His cause is a Church that is *katholikos*, or universal.

Now it is astonishing enough for me to meet with believers from Romania and Ethiopia and Zambia and Nepal and Ireland and to experience a bond that makes us feel as if we've known each other our whole lives long. It is amazing. But it was even more astonishing in the early generations of Christian faith, because nobody had ever seen anything like this before. Young and old. Wealthy and poor. Powerful and powerless. North Africans and Romans. Antiochenes and Alexandrians. All one Body responding to one calling.

So much is different today. Long eras of ineffectiveness of the churches of the world, scandals of leadership, strange mutations. But there is also an incredibly good story to be told. Today, people all over the world gather in churches with other believers who have found hope and life in Jesus Christ. They've found churches that are far from perfect but where love can be found. When Hurricane Katrina hit the United States, the most effective, most nimble organizations responding to the crisis were not government agencies but churches. There is still very good reason to say "I believe in the Church."

I believe in the communion of saints is a statement that takes believing in the Church a step further. It is to say that this association of people who believe in God as Father and Jesus as Savior and Lord and in the powerful presence of the Holy Spirit—which is the general meaning of "saints"—is not merely an association. It is a *communion*. A *community* sharing a *common* life, bearing a *common communication* between themselves and the world. This is a bond that connects the Ethiopian believer with the Romanian believer with the Argentine believer with the Chinese believer with the American believer. And the bond is not just with the living but also with the saints that have gone before, that are long deceased. When I read some of my favorite believing authors from past eras, it sometimes feels as if I know them better than the person living next door.

The opening words of 1 John put it as well as it can be put:

We proclaim to you what we have seen and heard, so that you also may have fellowship with us. And our fellowship is with the Father and with his Son, Jesus

Christ. We write this to make our joy complete. This
is the message we have heard from him and declare
to you: God is light; in him there is no darkness at
all. If we claim to have fellowship with him yet walk
in the darkness, we lie and do not live by the truth.
But if we walk in the light, as he is in the light, we
have fellowship with one another, and the blood of
Jesus, his Son, purifies us from all sin (vv. 3-7).

"Communion" means "fellowship," derived from the
Greek word *koinonia,* which is translated elsewhere in the
New Testament as "participation" (1 Cor. 10:16), "partner-
ship" (Phil. 1:5) and "sharing" (Phil. 3:10). It means spiritual
friendship; it also means the shared life. So when someone
says, "I believe *this*: I believe in the communion of saints," he
or she is saying, "I believe God has not left me alone in the
world. God didn't design me to live as if I occupied a desert-
ed island. God doesn't expect me to lose my loved ones and
grieve alone. God knows I'm not smart enough on my own
to figure life out. God has made me His child, so I have
brothers and sisters. I can learn from them. They can learn
from me. God is giving gifts into my life that He has first put
in the hands of other people. My voice does not need to sing
out to God in a solo of praise but a chorus of praise. And I
don't need to suffer alone."

The Church is not the only place where community can
be found, and when believers are on their worst behavior, a
church can develop into a dysfunctional group with tan-
gled relationships—hardly something that represents
Christ well in the world. But the Body of believers in Christ
holds the potential and has the mandate to be the most

fruitful, authentic, constructive community one can be part of. A "body" as the apostle Paul called it, where no member is unimportant, no ability is insignificant, where strong people support weak people, and are then support-ed by others when they take their turn at being weak (see Rom. 12:4-8).

My wife and I have been in a group with 10 other believ-ers that has met in our home every other Sunday night for discussion, sharing of need and wisdom, and prayer. It is a group of people who have gotten to know each other well—extremely well—given the fact that we've met in this way for the past 20 years. The group consists of men and women of various ages, different people with different interests and distinct (and strong) personalities. In the communion of this group, we have watched our children grow, have prayed for each other as loved ones became ill and died, have shared all the ups and downs of life. I always know that if I am off on a trip to California or China or Argentina, this group of people will have me in their minds and pray for me. Our bond is not the result of a program, a study guide or a leader. In fact, all of the people in the group are leaders in their spheres of influence, and when we get together we are one of the most leaderless groups you could ever see. It is a time to shift out of leader identity and just be people—so we stum-ble along, forgetting who is supposed to guide us through another quarter of meetings, forgetting who is supposed to bring the dessert this week and end up rummaging around in the freezer for some cookies left over from the last holiday. The bond is simply this: God has invited human beings to be part of His family, to live in His "household," and we see the benefits of that when we know our brothers and sisters.

We make a big mistake when we think of the Church as an institution—big, undefinable, abstract. God sees "the communion of saints" and invites us into a face-to-face connection with each other—communities that are personal and real. "Churches within churches," as someone put it many years ago. But because we human beings move so quickly to disappointing and damaging behavior, it will not be surprising if some can more easily say, "I believe in God the Father, and I believe in Jesus Christ, but I'm withholding judgment on believing in the Church." That's better than not believing at all. God is the object of our faith, not the Church. But we are invited to believe in the ideal of "the communion of saints" so that we don't relegate ourselves to a lonely, solitary spirituality—disconnected from the blessings of God through "the communion" and in no position to be a blessing to others.

I believe in *the forgiveness of sins*. Of all the things we want to believe, we really want to believe that we can be forgiven. Now that's not important to everybody, but I can't imagine why not. I guess some people figure that whatever hole they get into, they'll pull themselves out. Whatever injury they cause in someone else, the other person will just have to get over it. Whatever mistakes they make, they'll just try to do better next time. If they have a bad reputation with someone, that's too bad. If someone's angry with them for being a jerk, that's the other person's problem. It is as if such a person says, "If God is insulted with what I do in my life, if He can't look past my sins because there are other people who have sinned a lot worse than I have, well then . . . I'll just have to take my chances. What does God expect of me anyway?"

But the multitudes of people who have said these words, "I believe in the forgiveness of sins," believe that if God has provided a way of wiping the slate clean, giving them a fresh start, of taking the load of guilt off their shoulders, of making them blameless, then they want that. They want to believe that. And when they hear that what God expects is for them to admit their sins and fall on His mercy, then that is an offer they cannot refuse. They will give up their pride to give up their burden—in a minute. They believe in the forgiveness of sins.

Standing before a king to explain why he was perpetuating a radical new movement, the apostle Paul explained that Jesus had sent him to people "to open their eyes and turn them from darkness to light, and from the power of Satan to God, so that they may receive *forgiveness of sins* and a place among those who are sanctified by faith in [Jesus]" (Acts 26:18, emphasis added).

You could say there were many reasons why the early Jesus movement spread like wildfire, but one of the most compelling reasons was that when people heard that there was a way for them to be released from the nightmare of their regrets and failures—the things that make it difficult to sleep at night, the things that make the heart turn cold and hard—they said, in massive numbers, "We need that. We want that. We want to believe that." The early Christians knew they were delivering a revolutionary message. Not that love and mercy and forgiveness were not central to the message of the Old Testament, but as is often the case with human beings, the ideals get crusted over by self-made and self-aggrandizing forms of religion. What Jesus did was to crack the crust. His message of Kingdom and repentance was this: "God rules. You're trying to rule instead of Him. That's why you're in trouble. Change your mind, and you'll be released into the wide open skies of forgiveness."

Long after the Ceausescu regime in Romania was gone, the trials and sentencing of the merciless thugs of the Securitate began. My friend Mircea was brought in as a witness against the official who had beaten and abused him. On the witness stand, Mircea reminded the former colonel that he had said that the only God in Romania is the secret police. He asked the man, "Who is God in Romania?" The defendant's reply: "God is the only God in Romania."

Mircea agreed to answer the questions related to the trial and to provide information, but when the prosecutor of the case asked Mircea to plead with the judge for the strongest possible sentence against this man, Mircea declined. Somehow, he felt that his faith in Christ and the strength he had in Christ allowed him and required him to release this criminal to the judgment of the court, instead of he himself taking the role of judge. He told the judge, "I preach forgiveness from Scripture, and if I do not live it in my life then my preaching is worthless."

The judge sternly addressed the former colonel: "You should take off Mircea's shoes and kiss the soles of the feet that you beat. I wanted to condemn you for seven years, but this man forgives you."

That's the essential meaning of *forgiveness*: to release. We decide to release people from obligation or debt to ourselves—to the judgment of a higher court. Because our resentment and bitterness toward others can imprison us, we are invited to learn what it means to be forgiving people. That lesson begins with being forgiven ourselves—by God.

I believe in *the resurrection of the body, and the life everlasting.*

There is a doorway that faces us our whole lives. Sometimes we try to pretend it isn't there. Sometimes we give it an occasional glance. Sometimes we stare at it, maybe because of extreme age or terminal illness. That portal marks the line between this life and what lies beyond. Everybody crosses its threshold.

Now there are some who believe that the doorway opens to nothingness—blank air, a precipitous cliff. You just drop away.

Far more people believe in some form of life after death. And one of the most compelling explanations for that belief is that God has put eternity in our hearts (see Eccles. 3).

First Corinthians 15:35-37 talks about the "resurrection body," which means that life after death is not a melting into the universe but a renewed, personal, conscious existence. First Corinthians 15:42-44 says, "The body that is sown is perishable, it is raised imperishable; it is sown in dishonor, it is raised in glory; it is sown in weakness, it is raised in power; it is sown a natural body, it is raised a spiritual body." Revelation 21:1-6 talks about everlasting life—a quality of life that begins now but ends with "a new heaven and a new earth" (v. 1) where "the dwelling of God is with [people], and he will live with them. They will be his people, and God himself will be with them and be their God. He will wipe every tear from their eyes. There will be no more death or mourning or crying or pain, for the old order of things has passed away" (vv. 3-4).

The famous Roman emperor Marcus Aurelius, who saw himself as a refined philosopher/king, uncharacteristically lashed out against the Christians because he considered their beliefs superstitious and immoral. It was the middle of the second century and just a few generations after Jesus. Those were the days in Rome when it was a risky commitment to be baptized and confess in public, "I believe in God the Father Almighty; and in Christ Jesus His only Son, our Lord . . . and in the holy catholic Church, the bond of fellowship of believers, the forgiveness of my sins." And there was special poignancy to believing in "the resurrection of the body, and the life everlasting," because that doorway may be closer than you think. The doorway may be closer because you say "I believe."

They brought Polycarp, a leader of the Church, into the Circus Maximus. The crowds cheered and waited for the entertainment of seeing some more Christians killed by lions or turned into torches. It was entertaining to watch gladiators fight to the finish, but it was satisfying to the crowds to see scum like Christians torn apart, who often showed courage because of their strange beliefs, dying with their faces turned upward. Polycarp was 87 years old at the time. He was one of the few Christians on this date, A.D. 160, who was old enough to have personally known one of the original apostles—John, one of the Twelve, one of the three closest to Jesus, into whose care Jesus had entrusted His mother, Mary.

When agents were sent to arrest Polycarp, they were astonished that such an elderly and venerable man should be seen as a threat. All he needed to do was to acknowledge Caesar as Lord and the charges against him would be dropped. He refused.

In the Circus Maximus, it all became very real. The proconsul told him, "I have wild beasts that will tear you apart."

The old man said that changed nothing.

Then fire was threatened. "I can tie you to a stake and let the flames consume your flesh."

Still no change.

The crowds cheered as blocks and sticks of wood were piled up, as the old man was bound to the post, as the flames enveloped him. And we might think that the spectators walked away that day, as they had on other days when they saw Christians martyred, thinking, *Now there is one compelling reason* not *to believe.*

But at least one historian of the day pointed out that the cruel persecution of the followers of Christ had exactly the opposite effect on the populace. They became sympathetic. And as they witnessed believers pushed across the line between this life and the life to come—with faith and confidence—they were forced to wonder what they would do when they approached that line. It made them want to believe. And many did believe. Tertullian, a Christian writer of the day, put it this way: "The blood of the martyrs is seed."

I believe in the resurrection of the body, *and the life everlasting.*

I'm living a comfortable life right now in a country where my faith is not just tolerated but protected. The church where I serve is even given the benefit of being a tax-exempt organization. Nobody today is threatening to kill me for my faith, and I'm not aware of any disease that is working inside me. The doorway for me, for all I know, may be half a century away or tomorrow—I don't know. But I want to believe, with the same kind of certainty and strength that the martyrs had, in the resurrection of the body and the life everlasting.

CHAPTER 14

No More Excuses

He dropped out of high school at the age of 14 but became one of the most influential philosophers of the twentieth century, accomplishing what is rare for a philosopher: to be a teacher for multitudes of ordinary people. Mortimer Adler, born into an orthodox Jewish family in Brooklyn in 1902, dropped out to become a copy boy for the *New York Sun*. But in evening classes, he stumbled into a universe of ideas by reading the great works of Plato, Aristotle, John Stuart Mills, John Locke, and others. He started taking classes at Columbia University but never received his bachelor's degree, because he didn't get around to fulfilling his phys. ed. requirement. He studied year after year, however, until he was awarded a doctorate in philosophy, and he eventually became a professor at the University of Chicago. He became editorial chief for *Encyclopedia Britannica* (not bad for a high-school dropout) and edited the series *Great Books of the Western World*. He also co-founded the Center for the Study of the Great Ideas. Adler had little interest in writing for his fellow scholars. Almost everything he wrote was for ordinary readers, including one book called *How to Read a Book* and another called *Aristotle for Everybody*.

But what is really interesting about Mortimer Adler is that although his background was in orthodox Judaism, his specialty was the philosophy of the Middle Ages; and that meant he became an expert, really a world authority, on medieval Christian theology. And it was obvious to a lot of people who heard him speak about it that the more he delved into the history and theology of Christianity, the more sympathetic he was to it. He was actually inclined to believe it. He told people that he had been "on the edge of becoming a Christian several times"; and when asked why he didn't embrace Christian faith, he answered, "If one converts by a clear conscious act of will, one had better be prepared to live a truly Christian life. So you ask yourself, 'Are you prepared to give up all of your vices and weaknesses of the flesh?'"[1] He told one journalist that he had no intellectual barriers to Christian faith. His hesitation was about moral choices he wasn't yet willing to make.

At least Adler was honest. And he is clearly not the only person to come to believe that God the Father Almighty is real and that Jesus Christ is God's only Son, virgin born, crucified, resurrected, ascended—to come to believe all that and not to accept the Lordship of Christ. Why? Because receiving the free gift of God's salvation costs you the control of your life. Cling to your life and you'll lose it; lose it and you will find it.

When a person can say, "I want to believe—I really know I want to believe," and when that person finds a God who seems to be everything God should be, and this God's truth rings more loudly and clearly than anything ever has before, there still is a distance to cross to say "I believe." You can acknowledge a proposition at a distance, but accepting the Lord brings the matter right into the center of your life. And in between wanting to believe and really believing can stand

a multitude of thoughts and sentiments that add up to be—
well, to be honest—just excuses.

One of the most courageous things a person can do is to
go to God and say, "Dear Lord, no more excuses. I realize I've
been hiding behind one false reason after another, I've put
up one smoke screen after another, but I'm tired of doing
that. It is not honest to You, and I am less of a person for
hiding behind excuses. So I want to break free. I want to step
out, to commit. I want to really believe."

The epistle of Romans, which offers a step-by-step pro-
gressive explanation of the life with God, speaks about simple, essential belief in God:

> What may be known about God is plain to them
> [human beings], because God has made it plain to
> them. For since the creation of the world God's
> invisible qualities—his eternal power and divine
> nature—have been clearly seen, being understood
> from what has been made, so that men are without
> excuse. For although they knew God, they neither
> glorified him as God nor gave thanks to him, but
> their thinking became futile and their foolish hearts
> were darkened (Rom. 1:19-22).

Here is the essence: God has clearly made Himself
known (and the most important part is the implication:
He *wants* to be known), so people "are without excuse."
God has "made it plain." What we see in "what has been
made" is, first, the existence of God and, second, some of
the essential characteristics of God, like His power and His
divine nature.

When you walk into someone's home and your eye is drawn to a painting on a wall, you first of all assume that the art exists because of an artist. Paintings don't just appear on walls. And then you may perceive something about the personality of the artist—if the artist intended his or her anger or compassion or idealism to come through.

But here is the tragedy. In the same way that we ignore people who can be known and want to be known, human beings from the beginning of human history have known God superficially but then glanced away. We noticed that there must be a Creator, but we did not respond to Him as Lord and God. We often have not given thanks to God, so our whole way of thinking, the very structure of our thought life is futile and the light in our hearts has gotten dimmer and dimmer (see Eph. 4:17-19). The whole interior life has gone dark.

That's how you explain September 11, 2001. That's how you explain the Third Reich and Stalin and Pol Pot. But it's also how you explain the frequent waywardness of human beings on a less severe scale—the rancorous marriage, the estranged sibling, the gambling addiction.

Without excuse. God has shown Himself; He has spoken loudly; but we put up excuses. And its time for the excuses to go away.

Now if we're brave enough, we'll admit to this and take a careful look at our excuses. That's expecting a lot—but it is just the kind of dividing line between adolescence and adulthood that a young person takes when he or she concludes that excuses are no way to live. So what are some of the excuses we use to not accept and submit to the Lord we have actually come to believe in? Some of our excuses have to do with what we think about God and some about what we think about ourselves.

Excuse #1

*"I don't know if I can believe in God when I
see all the suffering in the world."*

For many people, the world's suffering is a personal barrier, and this is understandable. They may have watched a relative suffer a long, lingering disease and then death; they may have lost a loved one in an accident; or they may have visited a part of the world where there is suffering everywhere the eye can see. And God Himself does not want us to be so calloused as to be indifferent about suffering. So when I meet someone who expresses this reason for having trouble believing in God, I'm not all that interested in getting into a philosophical debate at that time—I want to know how that person is suffering. After all, God has compassion for those who suffer, even when they lash out at Him in their suffering.

But for some people, this is a philosophical barrier—and one that they let linger far too long. To hold God at arm's length, not doing the work of deeply thinking the whole matter through, is not only an insult to the Creator, but it is also a chasm we create between ourselves and the One we need most in the face of suffering.

The Bible makes it very clear that God is grieved when human beings take that most precious quality of freedom and turn it into an occasion for careless or destructive or aggressive behavior. The shortest verse in the Bible describes Jesus' reaction to the insult of a friend's untimely death.

Standing at the tomb of Lazarus, "Jesus wept" (John 11:35). This was not moist eyes or a melancholy tear tracing down His face. The Greek word for "wept" here implies anguish, a potent mixture of grief and anger. Jesus found death disgusting, and while He did not reverse many deaths as He reversed Lazarus's on that day, He stayed focused on His ultimate mission, which would liberate everyone who believes in Him from the ravages of death.

One reason why suffering in the world is not a good reason not to believe in God is that it solves nothing. We are no better off facing hurricanes or terrorism or disease alone than facing them knowing that a good and compassionate God is right there with us.

And then there is this: If suffering is a compelling reason *not* to believe in God, why is it that the sufferers themselves do not, generally speaking, turn away from God but turn toward Him? It always amazes me when I sit by the side of people trapped in a hospital or hospice bed, and as their body languishes, their faith brightens and sustains them. If the person had faith in God before the disease hit, he or she in most cases has a stronger desire to connect with God in his or her suffering. For some reason, sufferers usually do not blame God. Yes, they may cry out to God. They may use words similar to those in the psalms: "How long will this go on, oh Lord. Please don't abandon me. Save me in my hour of need" (see Pss. 6; 25; 27; 31; 71). But sufferers usually seem to know that they are better off suffering with God than without God and that there is no way that God really wanted them to end up where they are.

There also are multitudes of people who come to their final suffering, and the threshold of death can be seen not far away, and out of faith emerges hope—real hope. They come to the crossing line, not cursing God, but saying, not unlike Jesus, "Father, into your hands I commit my spirit" (Luke 23:46).

Excuse #2

"I think there must be many paths to God, so I don't know whether I can commit to one way."

Not being able to commit to one way of belief can come from the guilty conscience of not wanting to tell others that they are wrong. The thinking goes something like this: If you say that Christianity is right, then you're saying Hinduism and Buddhism and atheism are wrong; and you don't want to say that the person in the next cubicle at work or the person living across the street or your brother's wife is wrong (even though they may very well think *you* are drastically wrong). The problem with this reaction, which is highly subjective and personalized, is that it really prevents someone from engaging in any real search for truth. If you're afraid that when you find something true you're going to offend someone who disagrees with you, then you'll shrink away from the search. But that's no way to find God. And, for some, it is a convenient excuse—a way of not having to commit, not having to relinquish control.

When someone says to me that there must be many paths to God and that they have concerns about committing to one way, I tell them I can understand that and I don't think that by saying Jesus Christ is the way to God that you are saying that Muslims and Hindus and Buddhists are wrong in everything they say. There are all kinds of pathways that have been forged in an attempt to find God and to find ultimate meaning in life. Remember, we want to believe. But the real question is, What is the path that is going to complete the journey, the path that is going to get you out of the dark forest and back home where you belong?

If you've done much hiking, you know that you can be following a designated trail through the woods, until you come across a fork in the trail, one branch of which looks somewhat experimental in nature. Hikers before you have wondered, *Is that way, around to the left of the boulder, the continuation of the path or do I take that way that goes to the right?* You choose and then walk a ways ahead until the trail looks fainter and fainter and then is gone. And you realize that hikers before you have concluded they got off the path and returned to the fork and went the other way, relieved that the trail continued without fading away.

We human beings are, by nature, spiritual bushwhackers. That is why there are so many different religions in the world, all attempting to define a pathway to God. And the Christian doesn't (or shouldn't) criticize people for trying to find or forge a path. It is because of the irrepressible desire to search that we know that there is One worth searching for, a God who summons us. When the apostle Paul visited the culture-rich and intellectually stimulating city of Athens, he noted all the temples to different deities and, instead of condemning them, said to his Greek listeners, "I can clearly see how religious you and your city are. And I noticed one temple dedicated to an unknown God. Let me fill in the blank." And he proceeded to tell them about Jesus (see Acts 17:16-33).

Isn't it interesting that Jesus in His teaching didn't debate the dozens of different religions and philosophies of

His day? He spent virtually no time talking about what was *not* the way to God. What He did do is say, "I am the way and the truth and the life. No one comes to God the Father except through me" (John 14:6). And what He meant by that is not that He was the victor in the battle of religions; He was saying, "I have come from God the Father, I really have, and I intend to go ahead of you, defeating temptation, staring down Satan, clashing with the authorities, going into the coldness of death and coming out the other side—offering My hand to you to take you through it all. Now—will you believe that? And even if you don't understand all of it, will you suspend your excuses and trust Me?"

Excuse #3

"If God wants me to believe, He should show Himself."

The excuse of wanting to actually see God before believing is confronted specifically and directly in Romans 1:19-20. God *has* made Himself known. How? Through what He has made. What aspects of Himself has He made known? His "invisible qualities," like His power and His divine nature. Now this statement is clear and direct. Some things about God have been "clearly seen" and God made them "plain." You can't know everything about God by opening your eyes and looking at the stars in the sky and the teeming life of the earth, but you can know some things. And most important, you can know that God is real. So there is no excuse. Earth religions say you can know everything you need to know about God by looking at the creation (and that is because they equate God with the creation), and agnosticism says that there may be a God, but there is no way for us to really know that. Between these two extremes is this: For all time and all around the world, people have believed that there is a God, and they believe because it is plain and clear. There is a God. That God is divine—in other words, different from us, better than us. That God is powerful. He is a master designer. And if you acknowledge that, you are substantially on the way to believing.

Here is the challenge: No more excuses. No more halfway faith. No more invented gods made in the image our imaginations have dreamed up. No more excuses about God—that He's not doing enough or that He's not spoken clearly enough.

And no more excuses about ourselves.

Excuses #4 and #5

"I'm not bad enough to need God."
"I'm not good enough to deserve God."

Not being bad enough and not being good enough are two of the most common reasons people give for not letting go of their lives into the powerful hands of God—two excuses that flatly contradict each other. Now people may not use these exact words, but when you listen carefully to what people say, excuse #4 becomes very obvious. "I'm not bad enough to need God" is, for a lot of people, a little like saying, "No, doc, I don't need chemotherapy." Now the person with cancer may eventually acquiesce, of course, and seek the treatment. But for some people, it is easier to deny a dire diagnosis, even if there is an effective treatment at hand.

In my adolescence, it wasn't so much that I didn't believe in God, but I didn't think God was relevant. I believed I had gone through the appropriate rites of passage in the Christian religion. I had been baptized and then confirmed in the faith and generally had a positive sense of it all. But the thing that was twisted around in my thinking is that each step was a finishing rather than a beginning. I was moving toward an adulthood of having graduated from the Christian faith rather than being initiated into it.

But the main reason (or, to be more accurate, *excuse*) I treated God like a shadow at that stage of my life was that I didn't think I was so bad that I needed divine rescue. *It's not like my life is in the gutter,* I thought. (Although, in retrospect, I later realized I was dancing on the edge of the cliff.)

Most of us can easily answer this question: Are you more tempted to think that you're not bad enough to need God or that you're so bad you don't deserve God? Everybody leans one way or the other. When we take an honest look, a deep look, we may be surprised by what we find. And we never really know what is going on in the thinking of the people we live with and work with.

There is one person who thinks he is too good for God, but deep inside what is really going on is that he loathes himself and really thinks that God doesn't want to have anything to do with him. And next to him is someone who seems to be humble and even self-deprecating, but the reality is that he has a great deal of spiritual pride that is walling him off from God, thwarting what could be a healthy, flourishing spiritual life.

Some people's lives are written in big bold capital letters. That was the case with Johnny Cash, whose inner life was a tug-of-war between faith and failure. At the height of Johnny Cash's popularity, the most recognizable men on the planet were the president of the United States, the Pope, Billy Graham and Johnny Cash—and not necessarily in that order. For decades, Cash recorded one hit after another, and it all began with a meteoric rise in 1957 with the second and third songs he recorded with Sam Phillips of Sun Records. It was Cash, Elvis, Buddy Holly and Carl Perkins and the birth of rock 'n' roll. Cash thought he should take voice lessons so that he could sing better, but a voice coach told him to forget it. Improving his vocal ability would only ruin what quickly became one of the most recognizable voices in American culture.

But for all the success—sold-out concerts, hit records, cheering crowds (whether it was Madison Square Garden or Folsom Prison)—Johnny Cash carried with him a deep sense of loathing about who he was. It wasn't just that he became a drug addict and he felt guilty—he turned to drugs because he hated himself. He was frightened before every concert, thinking he was on the verge of failure.

On one dark day in October 1967, he decided he would end it all. It was the day to die. Time to get the anguish over; time to stop hurting other people. He went to the mouth of a cave on the Tennessee River where in the past he had looked for arrowheads and Civil War artifacts. Nickajack Cave was a deep system with twists and turns and side chambers and cliffs. He went in with a flashlight, determined to go farther and farther in until his batteries died and then lie down one last time. He crawled deeper and deeper, hour after hour, at least a mile into the complex labyrinth when the flashlight went out and he lay down in the darkness. Cash later wrote of that moment:

I was as far from God as I have ever been. My separation from Him, the deepest and most ravaging of the various kinds of loneliness I'd felt over the years, seemed finally complete.

It wasn't. I thought I'd left Him, but He hadn't left me. I felt something very powerful start to happen to me, a sensation of utter peace and sobriety. . . . There in Nickajack Cave I became conscious of a very clear, simple idea: I was not in charge of my destiny. I was not in charge of my own death. I was going to die at God's time, not mine.[2]

Cash began crawling in whatever direction seemed right. In the darkness he had to feel with his hands, crawling like a crab, lest he fall over a precipice. And then after a very long time, he felt a gentle breath of wind and knew that with the movement of air, there was a way out. He followed the wind until he saw the light and emerged. But he didn't emerge alone—there at the mouth of the cave was his mother and a friend waiting by his abandoned Jeep.

Years later, a photographer was taking photos of Johnny Cash when Cash's two dogs came up beside him. One was mostly black with a little white and the other was mostly white with a little black. Cash had named one Sin and the other Redemption. Cash explained that he kept the dogs as a reminder that none of us is completely good or completely bad.

"No more excuses" means not holding back. It means acting on that longing to believe that we all have, even if we still have unanswered questions or sentiments that create doubt. Any of us could wait until we have an answer to the problem of suffering or the plurality of religions before step-ping out in real faith and commitment. Any of us could remain lost in a dark cave of believing we'll never be good enough for God, and we have to become good enough to make headway with God. And any of us could think we'll do just fine in life without God.

Or we can do what we know we were created to do: believe.

Notes

1. "Conversation with an Author: Mortimer J. Alder, Author of *How to Think About God*," *Book Digest Magazine* (September, 1980), cited in Charles Colson, *Kingdoms in Conflict* (Grand Rapids, MI: William Morrow & Zondervan, 1987), p. 71.

2. Johnny Cash, *Cash: The Autobiography* (New York: HarperCollins, 1997), pp. 170-171.

CHAPTER 15

Way, Truth, Life

We live in a world in which there are many gods different people believe in. There is nothing new about that. Human beings have been searching for God since the beginning of creation. The religions of the world have come up with distinctly different answers to the same basic questions: What is the way, or path, my life should follow? What is true? How can I live? How long will I live? How should I live? Christians believe that faith in Jesus Christ as the way, the truth and the life gives ultimate answers to these ultimate questions. That phrase "way . . . truth . . . life" comes from Jesus' own mouth, at a defining moment in Jesus' teaching.

In the Upper Room where Jesus and His disciples shared a Passover meal on the night when Jesus would later be betrayed, arrested and put on trial, He told His inner circle of disciples that He would be leaving them, offering them words of comfort at the same time:

"Do not let your hearts be troubled. Trust in God; trust also in me. In my Father's house are many rooms; if it were not so, I would have told you. I am going there to prepare a place for you. And if I go and prepare a place for you, I will come back and take you to be with me that you also may be where I am. You know the way to the place where I am going."

Thomas said to him, "Lord, we don't know where you are going, so how can we know the way?"

Jesus answered, "I am the way and the truth and the life. No one comes to the Father except through me" (John 14:1-6).

The conclusion to Jesus' earthly ministry seemed so tragic—a very strange way to start a new religion. Of course, what Jesus was doing was not really starting a new religion but paving the way for human beings to be reconnected with their Creator, paying for the sins of the world. He had taught His disciples for three years and then told them, "I am leaving, and you know where I am going."

Now Thomas was the disciple who was always the best at asking questions. And his questions were honest, blunt and genuine. "Lord, we don't know where You are going, so how can we know the way?" Sometimes everybody in the room is relieved when one person asks the question everybody is thinking. Especially when everybody is troubled, when they sense something shadowy and foreboding in the air. Where *was* Jesus going? And *why*?

Imagine you are out on a hike in a deep dark forest. Your leader tells you he is going to leave and that you should stay on the way to get to the final destination. The only problem is, you don't recall having heard what the destination is; and not knowing that, you realize desperately that you have no idea which ravine you should follow, which stream you should cross, even whether you should be heading north, south, east or west. Without your leader, you know you are hopelessly lost. And that, of course, is exactly the point. That is why Jesus looked at His disciples and said to them, "*I am* the way." When you or I are trying to figure out the direction of our lives, the answer is not so much a "what" but a "who." Thomas's troubled heart is really no different from the troubled heart of any person. "Dear Lord, show me the path to follow."

We may ask the questions this way: What is the goal of my life? How do I get there? Is there a way—some way—out of my troubles? What is the purpose of my life?

Each of us needs to ponder what the real destination of life is and find that compelling answer. To have no idea where you are going in life is the essence of lostness.

Jesus claimed to be the path leading away from destruction and toward God and eternal life. Jesus did not say, "Here is a path" or "Here is the path," but "*I* am the path." Jesus and His disciples spent many days traversing Israel along dusty paths worn by hundreds of years of foot traffic. If you're on the path, you know you're okay. Get off the path into the dry, dusty desert, the wilderness, and you are lost.

For each of us, life is really a very long walk. Today you take just a few more steps. And if you are stepping toward God, there is this marvelous promise: You are stepping away from destruction because you are on "the way."

We need "the way" for every decision we make that is of a moral or spiritual character: Do I confront my cousin about how he is treating his wife? Do I let my grown-up kid move back home? How can I show love to my spouse? Should I take that new job? Should I make a change of career? How am I supposed to bear my cross today? A hundred questions and hundreds of possible answers, but only some answers are life-giving and right and honorable. Only some will keep me on the path leading to the final destination: reunion with God, coming to that new home that was designed to be our home from the start.

Now what about the issue of whether Jesus is the only way to God? This is a point of agitated conflict between Christians and non-Christians. Some would say that it is pure arrogance to say that Jesus is the only way to God. Others would say it just sounds confusing, because it would seem only fair to say that there are many different ways to God.

It should be pointed out, first of all, that most religions are exclusive in their claims. Hinduism does try to say that there are many paths leading up the same mountain, so one can follow the way of monotheism and polytheism and pantheism all at the same time. But most religions are quite specific in what they say. Islam, for instance, clearly states that there is only one God, and Muhammad is his mouthpiece, and the Koran is the only pure scripture.

What troubles me about these debates is that the premises are very often misunderstood. As a Christian, I believe that Jesus is the way to God. And when you say that, yes—you are saying something exclusive . . . but not *excluding*. There is a huge difference.

Christians do not say that Jesus is the way to God for the purpose of being exclusive and certainly not excluding. Any time a Christian has an attitude that wants to exclude, he or she is violating the very spirit of the message of Christ.

It's no wonder the rhetoric of Christian believers sometimes sounds strange to non-Christian ears. It sounds like someone saying, "I am in a privileged position. I take pride in drawing a boundary between you and me. My belief is dependent upon your exclusion. I am against you."

When someone says to me, "Do you really believe that Jesus is the only way to God?" my response is something like this: "I believe that Jesus is the way to God. I believe that Jesus did something utterly unique in the human race and for the human race. He died a death that was not merely martyrdom but atonement, the payment for the penalty of my sin. No one else has ever claimed to do that. The reason why the value of His death rises so far beyond martyrdom is because of who He is. I believe that Jesus is the Son of God, co-Creator of the world with God the Father, and that He existed before He came into the world in the family of a carpenter 2,000 years ago. I believe that human beings *should* have solved the problem of their guilt but only God *could*. That explains why the Son of God became a real person. Only God could provide the forgiving grace, and only God can change me from the inside out. Therefore, I believe that Jesus is, as He Himself said, the way to God. And because what He did was so completely unique in all of human history, yes, He is the only way to God. I don't believe this in order to exclude anybody but because my heart and mind have been taken captive by the love and power of God shown so convincingly in Christ's great work of rescue. And I'm thrilled that Jesus Himself extended His mercy and truth to anybody and everybody in the world. I will pass on the message of Jesus to anybody I can, because to do otherwise would only be selfishness on my part. And if someone receives this message and experiences for the first time in life the spiritual freedom that comes through Jesus, then that is not to my credit. In fact, it has nothing to do with me, even if I have transmitted the message. It is about one of God's beloved children making his or her way home."

Let's use a comparison here. Imagine you're at work in your office in a modern skyscraper. Suddenly the building is filled with smoke from a fire in some unseen part of the building. Though you thought you knew this building well, in the dense smoke you are disoriented, and you wander about for an exit, bumping into furniture and walls. Just then, a figure emerges from the smoke, wearing heavy dark clothing with fluorescent yellow stripes. By the boots and helmet and that tank on his back, you recognize him as a fireman. With an ax in one hand and a flashlight beaming from his helmet, he holds out his hand to you and shouts, "*Let me get you out of here!*" Now at that moment the most important reality of your life is that your rescuer has come. Because of who he is and what he is able to do, he knows far better than you how to get out of that building. You do not stand there and debate whether there are other ways out. You just follow him. You follow as closely as you can, not letting those florescent yellow stripes out of your sight for a moment. And he does get you out.

Christians believe that Jesus Christ is, as John the Baptist said of Him, "the Lamb of God, who takes away the sin of the world" (John 1:29), which is another way of saying that He made it possible for us to be truly and fully forgiven. He is not *a* lamb of God who takes away the sin of the world; He is not *one of* the lambs of God who takes away the sin of the world; He is *the* Lamb of God who takes away the sin of the world. The Bible says that God designed this rescue plan long before we were born or had our first major failure in life. It is up to us whether we look at God and say, "Thank You. I believe" or "I dare not believe that absolutely because it may appear that I am saying that somebody else is wrong."

This is not a philosophical debate over who can say they're right and who can say they're wrong. It is about rescue. The world is burning. We are all living in this world. There are some days that are bright and clear, and other days when we feel like we're groping our way through smoke-filled hallways.

What did Jesus mean when He said "I am the way"? Isn't it simply this: "Follow Me and you will be safe. Follow Me and you will be healthy. Follow Me and you will find God and you will find yourself, the true self God designed you to be"?

The next dramatic statement Jesus made about Himself to His disciples was that He is "the truth." It is hard to overstate how bold this claim is. It is bold to say, "I know the truth." In these days, it is even bold to say, "I believe there is truth." But when Jesus said "*I* am the truth," He was raising the issue to a whole new level. Remember, when Jesus said, "I am the way and the truth and the life," it was on the evening of that dividing line between His life and His death. Just hours later, after Jesus' arrest, He would stand before Pontius Pilate and say, "For this reason I was born, and for this I came into the world, to testify to the truth. Everyone on the side of truth listens to me" (John 18:37). And then came the chilling question of Pontius Pilate: "What is truth?" (v. 38).

Pilate's question may have been a cynical response, but it was the right question. And it remains the right question. It is why we do research, why we have universities, why we have publishing houses and why we have churches.

Now there are those who think that "What is truth?" is yesterday's question. That we have now grown up and we no longer look for the truth, because physics now presents us with different constructs of the universe that can apparently

be true at the same time and because historians are sup-
posedly always biased and because we certainly don't want
to get entangled with comparing the Christian faith with
other religions.

The problem is that this just does not square with everyday experience. We are continually looking for truth. The
only way to live is if you assume that there's a difference
between truth and falsehood. What if the bank sent you your
monthly statement with this disclaimer at the top: "This
statement may or may not be true." What if you were on trial
and the judge instructed the jury that they may or may not
prefer to seek the truth in their verdict? What if a candidate
for the office of president of the United States openly said in
the campaign that he or she was going to be selective on
which days he or she would tell the truth? What if you asked
your adolescent kid whether or not he or she was using
drugs—to give you the simple truth—and his or her response
was "What is truth?" What if you asked your doctor to tell
you the plain truth and he said to you, "I'm sorry, but our
hospital's policy is that we can choose whether or not to tell
patients the truth"?

None of us really believes that we've outgrown the need
for truth. None of us can live that way. So we should honest-
ly say that some of the things some religions teach are true
and other things are false. And when we read Jesus' words,
"For this reason I was born, and for this I came into the
world, to testify to the truth. Everyone on the side of truth listens to me" and "I am the truth," we should consider that
some of the best news the world has ever heard.

Now there is one important qualification to make here.
Christians believe that in Jesus Christ we have the eternal,

the utterly true, truth about God. But Christian faith does not require that a person say that all other religions in the world are wrong in everything they say. When the Muslim says, "There is only one God," the Christian should say, "Amen." When the Buddhist says, "We can do better than living as merely material creatures, only being concerned about the clothes we wear or the goods we amass," the Christian should say, "I agree with that." When the Hindu says, "God is mysterious to us," the Christian should not disagree. When the secular humanist says that human beings have fought shameful wars over religious convictions and have shed the blood of innocent people, and that is a crime, the Christian should say, "Sadly, I have to agree." When the Confucian says we need to be guided by wisdom and principle, the Christian can only say, "I believe in the principled life, too."

As someone has said, all truth is God's truth. It does not sharpen our understanding of the truth to believe that everybody who is not a Christian is wrong in everything they believe. The Christian believes that the truth of God is so substantial and so deep and so strong and so loud that it echoes across the centuries and throughout all cultures. Its strength does not come from our arguments, and its longevity does not depend on our institutions.

When I was in college, I had a wonderful professor of English literature who was something of a skeptic, who always wanted to keep me honest about my faith. So whether we were reading classical literature or Shakespeare, if there were biblical allusions, he would always ask me in front of the class to explain the connection. This was challenging, but I appreciated his blunt honesty. He often pointed out that in literature, there are numerous stories about a god becoming human and dying a sacrificial death only to rise again from death. And he believed that we should, therefore, understand Christianity and the story of Jesus as one more myth among many myths whose principals are honorable but still mythological.

The Christian writer C. S. Lewis, in a small essay called "Myth Became Fact," observed the same thing. But Lewis said that the fact that all other myths and other religions have stories that sound like the Christian gospel does not mean that the Christian gospel is myth. When something is so true, so boldly true, so obviously true, a primal truth, that truth echoes through human civilizations. It is as if human beings have known all along that they needed a sacrifice for their sins but that only a divine and human figure could do it. So we have the stories of mythology, which try to paint truth in the vivid colors of story. But in Jesus Christ, myth became fact. God really did it.

We need the truth about God the Creator. We need the truth about what this world is and how to live in it. We need the truth about ourselves. We need the truth about our created nobility and about our corruption and our fallenness. We need truth about our successes and our failures, our potential and our limitations, our honor and our shame. And God loves us enough to tell us the truth.

The third word of Jesus to His disciples was that He is "the life." The immediate concern on the mind of the disciples who traveled with Jesus was that He had told them that they were going to Jerusalem and that He would be turned over to the authorities who would put Him to death. "What do you mean you're going to die, Jesus? You have only just begun. There is so much proclamation to do, so many people to heal, so many preparations in order to throw off Roman oppression."

Within hours Jesus would be in the hands of His executioners.

There was another time when Jesus told His disciples that He was life. Jesus stood at the tomb of His friend Lazarus, and He sensed and expressed the insult of decay and death. He said, "I am the resurrection and the life. He who believes in me will live, even though he dies; and whoever lives and believes in me will never die" (John 11:25-26). And then He told the people to take away the stone at the entrance of the tomb. And He said in a loud voice, "Lazarus, come out!" (John 11:43).

In this world where there are so many gods, everybody is trying to come up with an answer about life and death. Some will say life is an illusion and so death is nothing either. Others will say you are simply a part of the cycle of nature, and you should not hope for anything more than the cycle of death and life that trees and frogs and melons go through. Some are betting on reincarnation, hoping to do better the next time around. Some religious fanatics believe that if you die a fiery martyr's death as a suicide bomber, paradise awaits you, full of virgins to do your bidding.

At the last supper in that Upper Room on the night He was betrayed, Jesus said He was "the way and the truth and the life," knowing that He was soon going to die a horrible physical death but that His death would be the means whereby we would live.

When I wrote the opening pages of this book, relating the story of my teenage daughter standing aghast in our driveway, looking at the burnt, smoking engine of her car,

I was able to write it with some amusement. I smiled when I remembered her saying that the engine sounded "like a thousand metal butterflies all flying at once." She knew there was something peculiar about the sound, but she didn't know the *meaning* of the sound.

I believe that this is the way we all are. Troublesome things happen in life, and disturbing headlines in almost every newspaper every day tell us that something is terribly wrong somewhere. But who will explain it? And is there any hope?

"A thousand metal butterflies" doesn't disturb me today because we were able to get that car fixed, and nobody was permanently damaged by the incident. And that is why I want to follow Jesus Christ my whole life. He explains the disturbing sights and sounds of life—and He lets us know how they can be fixed. That gives me hope.

What we are looking for today really isn't any different from what all human beings living in all places in the world have been looking for. The only real tragedy is when someone gives up looking for hope, when he or she stops saying, "I want to believe."

About the Author

Mel Lawrenz has authored or co-authored seven books, including *Patterns: Ways to Develop a God-Filled Life*. He has been a pastor at Elmbrook Church in Brookfield, Wisconsin, for the past 27 years, succeeding Stuart Briscoe as senior pastor in 2000.

Mel was born in Chicago in 1955 and grew up in Green Bay and Ellison Bay, Wisconsin. He earned his B.A. in creative writing at Carroll College, his M.Div. at Trinity Evangelical Divinity School, and a Ph.D. in historical theology at Marquette University. During the past 20 years, Mel has also taught as an adjunct faculty member at the University of Wisconsin in Milwaukee, Wisconsin, and at Trinity Evangelical Divinity School.

Mel hosts a weekly radio interview program called *Faith Conversations* and maintains an innovative and interactive website at www.cometobrook.org, which features streaming interviews, articles, resources, and more.

Mel married his high-school girlfriend, Ingrid, in 1975, and they have two college-aged children. Mel's personal interests include almost anything that will get him outdoors, particularly if it's near a body of water.